"McGrane's reflections, analogies to contemporary events or medical practice, and suggestions for prayerful reflection will encourage those who are suffering, their families and caregivers to better understand the spiritual value of suffering and thus be united more closely with God."

Jean R. Bostley, S.S.J.
Catholic Library Association

"It is rare that we get a glimpse of our saints and heroes in their full physical and emotional humanity. By giving focus to illness and disability in the real human lives of saints, *Saints to Lean On* is a stunning exposé of eleven individuals who faced the same difficult physical and emotional conditions we and our loved ones face. Our tendencies to spiritualize every aspect of a saint's life can alienate us who live in our bodies from drawing near and finding companionship with the saints. McGrane masterfully reveals the experience and meaning of illness and disability in her life and the lives of these saints and offers us companions worth befriending for life!"

Kathleen M. Schipani, I.H.M.
Pastoral Care for Persons with Disabilities
Archdiocese of Philadelphia

"...an interesting new twist on the lives of the saints. McGrane shares important insights into the redemptive mystery of suffering....I recommend this book to anyone who has questioned why people must suffer—whether they themselves are experiencing suffering or are concerned on behalf of a friend or loved one."

Janice L. Benton, S.F.O.
Executive Director
National Catholic Partnership on Disability

# saints
# to lean on
*Spiritual Companions*
### for illness
### and disability

JANICE McGRANE, S.S.J.

## ST. ANTHONY MESSENGER PRESS
Cincinnati, Ohio

Excerpts from *Almost Home: Living with Suffering and Dying*, directed by David Howard, copyright ©1989, used with permission of Liguori Publications, Liguori, MO, 63057, 1-800-325-9521, www.liguori.org. Excerpts from *Catherine of Genoa: Purgation and Purgatory, The Spiritual Dialogue*, Serge Hughes, trans., copyright ©1979, used with permission of Paulist Press, Inc., New York/Mahwah, NJ, www.paulistpress.com. Excerpts from *The Gift of Peace*, by Joseph Cardinal Bernardin, copyright ©1997, used with permission of Loyola Press, 1-800-621-1008, www.loyolabooks.org. Excerpts from *The Letters of Caryll Houselander: Her Spiritual Legacy*, Maisie Ward, ed., copyright ©1965, and *A Rocking-Horse Catholic*, by Caryll Houselander, ©1955, used with permission of Sheed & Ward, an imprint of Rowman & Littlefield Publishers, and by Continuum International Publishing Group. All rights reserved. Excerpts from *Matt Talbot and His Times*, by Mary Purcell, ©1954, used by permission of Gill & Macmillan, Dublin, Ireland. Excerpts from *My Brother Joseph: The Spirit of a Cardinal and the Story of a Friendship*, by Eugene Kennedy, copyright ©1997, used with permission of St. Martin's Press. All rights reserved. Excerpts from *Other Apostolates Today*, and "In Him Alone Is Our Hope," by Pedro Arrupe, copyright ©1984, used with permission of the Institute of Jesuit Resources, St. Louis, MO. All rights reserved. Excerpts from *Revelations of Divine Love*, Roger Roberts, ed., copyright ©1982, used with permission of Continuum International Publishing Group. Excerpts from *Sister Thea Bowman, Shooting Star: Selected Writings and Speeches*, Sister Celestine Cepress, ed., copyright ©1993, used with permission of the author. Excerpts from *St. Thérèse of Lisieux: Her Last Conversations*, John Clarke, O.C.D., trans., copyright ©1977, used with permission of ICS Publications, 2131 Lincoln Rd., N.E., Washington, DC 20002-1199, www.icspublications.org.

The Scripture quotations contained herein are from the *New Revised Standard Version Bible*, copyright ©1989 by the Division of Christian Education of the National Council of the Churches of Christ in the U.S.A. Used by permission. All rights reserved. (Note: The editors of this volume have made minor changes in capitalization to some of the Scripture quotations herein. Please consult the original source for proper capitalization.)

Cover and book design by Mark Sullivan
Cover photo ©istockphoto.com/Allan Brown

LIBRARY OF CONGRESS CATALOGING-IN-PUBLICATION DATA
McGrane, Janice, 1949-
Saints to lean on : spiritual companions for illness and disability / Janice McGrane.
p. cm.
Includes bibliographical references.
ISBN-13: 978-0-86716-595-1 (pbk. : alk. paper)
ISBN-10: 0-86716-595-2 (pbk. : alk. paper) 1. Christian patron saints—
Biography. 2. People with disabilities Biography. 3. Sick—Biography. I. Title.

BX4656.5.M24 2006
282.092'2—dc22
[B]

2006015031

ISBN-10: 0-86716-595-2
ISBN-13: 978-0-86716-595-1

Published by St. Anthony Messenger Press
28 W. Liberty St.
Cincinnati, OH 45202
www.AmericanCatholic.org

Printed in the United States of America

Printed on acid-free paper

07 08 09 10 5 4 3 2

*In Memory of*
*Liam Charles McGrane*
*1997–2002*

li

Laughing
boy-child

you play now
among the angels,

dancing forever
in God's heart
and
ours.

li

## acknowledgments

I express deep gratitude for assistance and support to Kathleen Rooney, S.S.J., for her faith in me and in this book; John Bernardine, S.S.J., for her every good work; Ann Edward, S.S.J., and Dr. Jane Mueller for invaluable editing assistance.

Special thanks to Bob and Carol Jensen, Edie and Tom McGarrity, my mother, Trudy, my deceased father, Tom, and my siblings, Joan, Karyn, Tom and Maureen, Mary Jo Larkin, S.S.J., and the staff at Chestnut Hill College Library, V. O'Keefe, S.J., Dorothy Ann Kundinger, F.S.P.A., Charlene Smith, F.S.P.A., Marla Lang, F.S.P.A., Jean Kasparbauer, F.S.P.A., Deacon Paul Gallagher, M. McKeever, S. Moore, K. Lunn and M.A. Silverman.

And also to the following Sisters of St. Joseph: A. Bucci, J. Ballerino, S. Kennedy, Rose Christine, K. Donohue, M. Pfaff, M. Rosarii, J. Berk, C. Nerney, N. Gaitley, K. Miller, M. Aherne, J. Riethmiller, F. Hall, Ann V. Snyder, J. Walsh, Clare Leona and C. Griffin.

# contents

Introduction · · · · · · · · · · · · · · · · · · · · · · · · · · · · · · · · · · · · · · · · · · · ix

Note to Readers · · · · · · · · · · · · · · · · · · · · · · · · · · · · · · · · · · · · · · · · · xiii

One · · · · · · · · · · · · · · · · · · · · · · · · · · · · · · · · · · · · · · · · · · · · · · · · · · · · · 1
· BLESSED MARGARET OF CASTELLO, *Our Companion in Multiple Disabilities*

Two · · · · · · · · · · · · · · · · · · · · · · · · · · · · · · · · · · · · · · · · · · · · · · · · · · · 15
· JULIAN OF NORWICH, *Our Companion in Serious Illness*

Three · · · · · · · · · · · · · · · · · · · · · · · · · · · · · · · · · · · · · · · · · · · · · · · · · 27
· SAINT CATHERINE OF GENOA, *Our Companion in Caregiving*

Four · · · · · · · · · · · · · · · · · · · · · · · · · · · · · · · · · · · · · · · · · · · · · · · · · · 39
· SAINT IGNATIUS LOYOLA, *Our Companion in Temporary Disability*

Five · · · · · · · · · · · · · · · · · · · · · · · · · · · · · · · · · · · · · · · · · · · · · · · · · · 51
· BLESSED KATERI TEKAKWITHA, *Our Companion in Physical Disfigurement*

Six · · · · · · · · · · · · · · · · · · · · · · · · · · · · · · · · · · · · · · · · · · · · · · · · · · · 67
· SAINT THÉRÈSE OF LISIEUX, *Our Companion in Terminal Illness*

Seven · · · · · · · · · · · · · · · · · · · · · · · · · · · · · · · · · · · · · · · · · · · · · · · · · 81
· VENERABLE MATT TALBOT, *Our Companion in Alcoholism*

Eight · · · · · · · · · · · · · · · · · · · · · · · · · · · · · · · · · · · · · · · · · · · · · · · · · 95
· CARYLL HOUSELANDER, *Our Companion in Mental Illness*

Nine · · · · · · · · · · · · · · · · · · · · · · · · · · · · · · · · · · · · · · · · · · · · · · · · · 109
· CARDINAL JOSEPH BERNARDIN, *Our Companion in Cancer*

Ten · · · · · · · · · · · · · · · · · · · · · · · · · · · · · · · · · · · · · · · · · · · · · · · · · · 123
· SISTER THEA BOWMAN, *Our Companion in Joy-Filled Suffering*

Eleven · · · · · · · · · · · · · · · · · · · · · · · · · · · · · · · · · · · · · · · · · · · · · · 139
· FATHER PEDRO ARRUPE, *Our Companion in Stroke*

Bibliography · · · · · · · · · · · · · · · · · · · · · · · · · · · · · · · · · · · · · · · · · · 153

Notes · · · · · · · · · · · · · · · · · · · · · · · · · · · · · · · · · · · · · · · · · · · · · · · · · 157

*I*llness always has been, and always will be, part of the human condition. Illness and disability—from an attack of the flu to the chronic conditions of cerebral palsy and multiple sclerosis to the final journey of a terminal disease—are unavoidable parts of life.

Yet illness, as well as the many other forms of human suffering, retains within its shell of pain and struggle the seeds of sanctity. Inherent in the struggle with illness and disability is grace: that mystical gift of God that empowers us and helps us to grow. It is when we are open to this mystical gift that the very vehicle of its giving—the illness itself—becomes sanctified.

It is not surprising then that the mystics and saints of Christian spirituality almost always experienced illness at some point in their lives. Ignatius of Loyola's conversion occurred while he was recuperating from a serious leg wound. Julian of Norwich's visions of Jesus came while she was thought to be dying. Thérèse of Lisieux suffered agonies while dying of tuberculosis at the tender age of twenty-four, yet she exhibited the radical trust in God that was so vital to her spirituality. Indeed, it is difficult to find a saint or a mystic whose life has *not* been touched significantly by disability or illness. What can we learn then from the lives of these men and women who have dealt with illness or disability? How can they be companions to us? Can each of them truly be someone we can lean on?

It is my sincere hope that you, readers of this book who cope with illness or disability, will find in its stories not only inspiration and someone with whom to identify, but also spiritual companionship. On those days when coping with your own life situation seems not only difficult but lonely, turn to Julian of Norwich or Thea Bowman, who knew serious illness and disability well. In prayer speak to them from your heart and know that they are eager to accompany you.

My own life with illness prompted me to write this book. When I was twenty-five years old, happily teaching high-school English, I began to wake up every morning with stiffness in my hands and legs. The diagnosis was startling: rheumatoid arthritis, a condition I had barely heard of and erroneously believed only older people could get. Thus my own journey with chronic illness and disability began.

I am fortunate that, due to improved medications complemented by nutritional supplements, my disease is now in remission. However, I remember well the difficult moments: lying on a gurney waiting to be operated on, or listening to my doctor reluctantly telling me the disease was spreading to a new part of my body. Often during these dark times I wondered how the God whom I *knew* loved me could allow this to happen. It was in those challenging moments that I remembered the example of radical trust that Thérèse of Lisieux, my spiritual companion and role model, had exhibited so frequently during her own illness. I prayed for that same grace of radical trust.

After years of struggle and prayer, I have concluded that life was never meant to be a rose garden; that suffering, whether in the form of illness, deep grief, addiction or physical or emotional pain of any sort, is simply a part of life. However, the constant invitation in any form of suffering is to know that God is with us. God was with me in my trips to the operating room and is with me as I write this right now. Jesus has kept his promise at the end of the Gospel of Matthew: "I am with you always, to the end of the age" (28:20).

My journey from the anger and frustration of "Why me?" to "Why not me?" has been both deeply blessed and immensely challenging, but marked by the absolute assurance that God has accompanied me closely in every movement and every breath. I am also convinced that God has made good use of my illness and resulting disability. My physical condition enables me to minister "with," not "to," other people who also live with disabilities. After working in two dioceses for seventeen years, ministering with people with disabilities and illnesses of every kind, I became aware of the deep spiritual needs of the people with whom I ministered. In my experience, like Joseph Bernardin, people with illness or disability first need to resolve the ever-important "Why?" question. Like Julian of Norwich, they need to find the spiritual meaning in living with illness. Also, they need to know the profound spiritual power of the redemptive aspect of suffering, as Caryll Houselander so often stressed.

Finally, there is the great challenge of the example of Margaret of Castello: to realize the impact that persons with significant disabilities have on nondisabled people. It gives tremendous witness to the transforming power of suffering when those of us with significant disabilities are open to the grace of accepting our conditions and are able to declare with pride, "Yes, this is who I am in God."

A word about the eleven "spiritual companions" about whom I chose to write. I chose these individuals for their personal appeal. Not only did I find their journeys compelling, but I also found that their writings and their powerful witness to others demonstrated great spiritual lessons on how to live with debilitating illness or disability.

It is in this spirit of companionship with the holy people of God, both living and dead, that I offer this book. Anyone who has ever coped with a disability or illness, anyone who cares about someone with a disability or illness, or is interested in the lives of saints, will find the stories, the strength and the spirituality of the eleven saints discussed in this work inspiring and hope-filled. While each of these remarkable individuals experienced the very human struggles and frustration of illness or disability, they also responded to the grace of God.

So how, precisely, do we begin to cultivate a friendship with someone among the communion of saints? In the same way we develop earthly relationships. First, get acquainted. Read the person's biography or books or commentaries about her or him. The *Catholic Encyclopedia*, Butler's *Lives of the Saints* and Robert Ellsberg's *All Saints* are all good places to begin. Next, engage in prayerful conversation with this friend. Don't be afraid to pour out your heart, to ask questions or to request intercession before God. Then, open your heart and listen closely for a response. Also, it can be helpful to use your imagination to picture your saint encouraging and accompanying you.

Keep alert for the subtle ways your heavenly friend may be attempting to connect with you. Notice such "holy coincidences" as hearing someone speak about your spiritual friend, finding your saint's prayer card in an old book, or simply experiencing a deep inner conviction that he or she is present.

In a culture that worships strength, beauty and productivity, living with a chronic condition of any sort is indeed challenging. After years of ministering with many people who lived with tremendous physical losses, I am convinced that illness can indeed become truly holy, containing the potential for tremendous spiritual power. The realization of the redemptive nature of suffering, the opportunity to see the sacred in the mundane, the invitation to make the illness a prayer—all these are graces for which to pray. As those of us who are "there" know well, living with illness or disability can at times be a very lonely and isolating experience. How comforting it is to know that the communion of saints have not only preceded us in dealing with difficult physical and emotional conditions, but are extending loving, helping hands to us, longing for the moments when we reach back and say "yes" to their offers of friendship and love.

_W_hen speaking of saints, I offer one caveat for the Catholic reader: We must be careful of our phrasing when talking about our prayer and saints. Invariably, we say that we pray "to" a certain saint. Praying "to" saints was one factor that led to the Protestant Reformation, and rightly so. For ultimately, _it is only God who has the power to answer our prayers._ While we really mean that we pray and ask the saints to pray "with us" to God, our phrasing suggests that we believe that God's divine power is shared by all in heaven. This is not what the Scriptures or the Catholic church teaches.

Praying "with" a saint or "with" a deceased loved one implies a great spiritual truth: that the cords of death do not destroy the bonds of love. Thus we pray, talk and commune "with" the saints, including those among our own family and friends, aware that although they now dwell in another realm, they are still present to us.

_History of Sainthood_
Belief in the communion of saints is among the most ancient of Christian traditions. In the Apostles' Creed, the earliest Christian creed, the church stressed its deep belief in the communion of saints by placing it immediately after the phrase "the holy Catholic Church."

The earliest Christians considered *every* baptized person, living or dead, a saint. Soon they began to recognize that some of their numbers, especially those who had died for their Christian beliefs, were worthy of particular veneration and imitation. Cults, or followings, began to spring up around certain saints. Heaven was likened to an earthly Roman court, where a patron could plead for assistance to the king. Thus began the practice of asking a particular saint to intercede for a specific intention.

As the church evolved over the centuries, the method of canonization, or declaring someone a saint, became more structured and systematized, although the process was always initiated as a result of popular acclaim from the people. (For further information on the history and politics of the canonization process, consult *Making Saints* by Kenneth Woodward.) Eventually, more formalized procedures began to be implemented for papal canonization, requiring a proponent (or postulator) for a certain individual's cause, as well as an opponent (or defender of the faith, also known as the "devil's advocate"). A certain number of miracles was required for the stages of veneration, beatification and canonization. Most recently, Pope John Paul II dropped the role of devil's advocate and decreased the number of miracles required for canonization. During his pontificate, he canonized over six hundred new saints, far surpassing his predecessors in saint-making.

Devotion to the saints declined drastically in the second half of the twentieth century, to the detriment of our collective cultural spirituality. In *Friends of God and Prophets* theologian Elizabeth Johnson aptly points out: "[T]he clear and easy trafficking between heaven and earth enjoyed by early Christian and medieval ancestors in the faith has broken down."[1] The reasons for this are many: the skepticism and secularism of today; the assimilation into the American mainstream of most European immigrant cultures, each with its own special patron saints; the decline of interest in organized religion and religious devotions in general; and the erroneous belief that the saints are too perfect and distant for us to identity with. However, since the 1990s there has been a resurgence in interest in the communion of saints: books are being written, calendars published and homilies given about them. We are reclaiming an important part of our Christian heritage. We need our friends in heaven. We need their example, their prayers with and for us and their stories. Most of all, we need their companionship.

Johnson refers to the communion of saints as "a Christian symbol that speaks of profound relationship."[2] Her book unearths the *relationship* model for the communion of saints that was prevalent in the early church: "[T]he saints are not situated *between* God and living disciples, but are *with* their sisters and brothers through the one Spirit poured out in the crucified and risen Jesus Christ."[3] This model of companionship is indicated by the fact that the saints are known as a *communion*—a word which clearly implies interaction, connectedness and sharing. The earliest Christians viewed their deceased loved ones not as intercessors, but rather as friends in heaven. These heavenly friends not only understood the struggles and temptations of being human, but also shared the same faith and hope in the living God.

## one

BLESSED MARGARET OF CASTELLO
*Our Companion in Multiple Disabilities*
(1287–1320)

*I*t is the year 1287. A baby girl is born in Italy with multiple disabilities, to the revulsion of her aristocratic parents. They hastily cancel the celebration of the birth of their heir, hide her away, and announce that the child has died.

It is the year 1963. Baby M is born in Johns Hopkins Hospital with Down's syndrome, to the revulsion of his middle-class family. His parents refuse to authorize life-saving surgery for their son's additional minor medical condition, an intestinal blockage. The infant is placed in an out-of-the-way room in the hospital and allowed to die of starvation.

The life of Blessed Margaret of Castello has much to say to us today. We think we are far removed from cruel medieval mindsets; yet, as the story of Baby M demonstrates, some people still place expediency over human life, throw away children with disabilities, both born and unborn, permit doctors to destroy life rather than preserve it and allow hundreds of thousands of people to live on the streets. The story of Margaret of Castello illustrates clearly why every human life, no matter how weak, frail, poor or disabled, is God's handiwork and is to be cherished and valued.

Long before there was a disability rights movement, Margaret of Castello demonstrated how a person with many disabilities, a woman who could easily be as marginalized in our day as she was in her own, can instead live a happy, productive, holy life. A life that says a resounding "no" to those who want to abort babies with or without disabilities. A life that models how to live joyfully within limitations. A life that glorifies God. A life that celebrates life.

### Margaret's Parents

Thirteenth-century Italy was a fledgling nation-state, experiencing continual warfare among its various regions. Margaret's parents, Lord Parisio and Lady Emilia, were members of the upper echelons of the Italian nobility. Interestingly, their family name has never been revealed; perhaps it was deliberately obscured by Margaret's biographers because of her parents' appallingly cruel treatment of their daughter.

In medieval days the fate of a royal marriage and the stability of entire countries rested on the ability of a noble couple to produce a male heir. Parisio and Emilia had hoped for a son to be their heir. A successful military man, Parisio longed for a son to follow in his footsteps and inherit his estate in Metola, Italy. He and his wife carefully planned a large feast to celebrate the birth of the next lord of the castle of Metola.

### Margaret's Birth and Early Years

As Lady Emilia's time to give birth approached, the castle of Metola busily prepared for a huge celebration of the hoped-for son. But soon after the guests had arrived, they were abruptly told to depart and the banquet was canceled. For, to the deep sorrow of Emilia and Parisio,

God gifted them not with the son they so eagerly sought but with a baby daughter. As well as being of the wrong gender, their newborn daughter disappointed them in other ways: She was born with many physical disabilities. The tiny infant was blind and short of stature. She had a form of what is now known as scoliosis, a curvature of the spine. In addition to all this, her right leg was considerably shorter than her left, and, perhaps worst of all to her pretentious parents, she had facial deformities. Her angry and disappointed parents recoiled in horror from their tiny child and announced that she had died. They then hid her away in the castle, placed her in the care of servants and had almost nothing to do with her.

As so often happens, however, God had different plans for this little girl with multiple disabilities. A maid baptized her, naming her Margaret (meaning "pearl"). As Margaret grew, she strolled haltingly about the castle but was hastily hidden away by her parents whenever visitors came. Her parents had little time for her, keeping her in the care of the servants. Padre Capellano, the chaplain of the castle, instructed the young girl in the Catholic faith. He sensed Margaret's desire to grow closer to God. Padre Capellano tried to tell Margaret's parents about her spirituality but was rebuffed.

Rejection by a parent is painful for any child, and this was rejection in every sense of the word. Margaret was to stay out of her parents' sight, out of their lives, even out of their living quarters, lest their noble friends see her and suspect her identity. But Margaret was blessed with tremendous coping skills—skills that are vital for any person with a disability of any time or place. She found solace in the servants of the castle, who responded to her warm, loving nature and grew quite fond of her. As the years went by, the servants saw her loving heart before they saw her limp or her blindness. This was to be a defining characteristic of Margaret of Castello's life: a loving personality that encouraged others to love her for her gifts, rather than reject her for her disabilities.

*Short Stature*

Margaret indeed had a significant level of disability. She grew, but she remained short in stature, considerably smaller than other children her age. This is a difficult disability. Persons of unusually short stature, who were once referred to as "dwarves," meet physical obstacles that average-sized individuals do not, as the world is geared to persons of normal height. But that is nothing compared to the scorn and ridicule that persons of short stature experience in a society in which many people worship physical beauty and strength. I once attended a concert with Julie, an intelligent, sensitive woman of short stature. Wherever we went, people pointed at, laughed at and made rude remarks directed at my friend. I was appalled, but Julie, accustomed to this treatment, continued calmly walking and conversing as though nothing were happening. Margaret of Castello no doubt had similar experiences.

Besides her short stature, one of Margaret's legs was shorter than the other, causing her to limp. She must have had difficulty navigating the dirt and flagstone floors of the castle of Metola and later the unpaved streets of Castello. Depictions of Margaret always show her with a cane or walking stick.

*Blindness*

Today, with the help of guide dogs, computers and other assistive technology, many people who are blind are able to live fully functioning and self-supporting lives. Programs help people who have vision loss adapt to their environment. Descriptive Braille tags are sewn into clothing to help people who are blind dress properly. They also fold their money in different ways to denote different denominations and wear watches that voice the time at a push of a button.

In the thirteenth century, however, persons who were blind found their way around as best they could, and were often forced to beg for a living. With her quick intelligence Margaret, despite her blindness, soon learned the many winding passages and nooks and crannies of the castle and got around quite well. But an incident that occurred when Margaret was six years old removed her forever from her secure home in the castle.

### The Discovery

One day, young Margaret, on her daily stroll about the castle, unexpectedly met a noblewoman who was visiting Margaret's mother, Lady Emilia. A maid intervened before the visitor could discover that this child with many disabilities was actually the daughter of the hostess. However, the incident frightened Margaret's noble parents so much that they resolved it would never happen again.

Lady Emilia wanted to place Margaret far away in the mountains with a peasant family. But her father, the "noble" Lord Parisio, had a different plan. Padre Capellano had often told the couple of their daughter's deep inclination toward God and toward prayer. They resolved to put Margaret in a place where she would be able to pray continually and where her true identity as their daughter would never be discovered. Accordingly, Parisio made his daughter into a recluse.

### "Put Away"

Today families of children with disabilities are sometimes encouraged to institutionalize their children. This was not an option in Margaret's day. However, retirement from the world to live a life of prayer and sacrifice was not uncommon in medieval times. In all cases, however, this lifestyle was freely chosen by adults who sought to live deeper spiritual lives. The life of an anchorite, however, was never intended for a child. Parisio used Margaret's spiritual inclination and love for God as an excuse to imprison her somewhere out of the castle, in a place where there would be no risk of discovery.

Parisio ordered a stonemason to construct a small, low-ceilinged enclosure attached to the local church, located in the mountains a few miles from the castle. Through one window was a view of the altar of the church; through the other window, food was passed to Margaret.

The room was bitterly cold in the winter and stiflingly hot in the summer. For the next thirteen years, Margaret lived there in solitude, with only the birds and the mountain wind for companions.

How could a young child survive in a small, damp room, deprived of parental love and human contact? Would this not be enough to render her deeply bitter if not insane?

Margaret's own family's rejection of her has also been experienced by persons with disabilities throughout the centuries and still even in our own day. As mentioned earlier, parents are sometimes still advised to institutionalize their children with disabilities. The removal of older children with disabilities from the family home is all too common. Institutional life is notorious for disregarding individual needs and stressing conformity and expediency. Until a few years ago, some institutions for persons with mental retardation would extract their residents' teeth in order to expedite feeding them liquid meals through funnel-like tubes. Such inhumane treatment spawned the effort to place people with disabilities in group homes located in the community rather than in impersonal institutions.

Margaret was deprived even of the human contact that an institution would have provided. Her companions were the foxes and the birds, and the plenteous fir trees that carried the mountain breezes to her small cell. Margaret loved God dearly. Her life in the castle was imbued with the doctrine and faith of the Catholic church. She was able to hear Mass and receive the sacraments, and Padre Capellano was able to visit her. These, along with her deep faith in God and her prayer life, greatly helped Margaret endure the hardships and isolation of her enclosure.

### Margaret's Final Abandonment

Margaret's life took an abrupt turn when she was nineteen and her parents, Emilia and Parisio, reached the nadir of their "parenting." Hearing that healing miracles had occurred at the tomb of Fra Giocoso, a lay Franciscan friar, in nearby Cite die Castello, they took

Margaret there. In September of 1306 they set out on the arduous journey over the Apennine Mountains to Castello. One cannot help wondering how they would have presented their formerly hidden, now nineteen-year-old daughter to their aristocratic friends had she actually been healed.

Unfortunately for Emilia and Parisio, Margaret was not healed of her multiple disabilities. God's refusal to meet their demand was the last straw. Once certain there was to be no miracle, they left their daughter exactly where she was—praying at the tomb of Fra Giocoso. They abandoned her to the streets of Castello and returned to their castle, never to be threatened again by the "shame" of a severely disabled daughter. They never saw Margaret again.

At the age of nineteen, Margaret, blind and short of stature, became a homeless person. Totally alone and totally unprepared, she was now to fend for herself on the streets of Castello.

*Life on the Streets*
Living on the streets of a medieval town was daunting. The streets were unpaved and unsanitary, with garbage, horse droppings and the contents of chamber pots everywhere. The streets were also dangerous: Thieves, beggars and bands of unsavory characters roamed about unchallenged. Women were vulnerable to sexual predators. And, of course, there were no soup kitchens, shelters or programs to assist homeless people.

For Margaret, these dangers were aggravated by her lack of sight and her other disabilities. She had to learn the streets and byways of Castello on her own and how to eke out a living by begging for alms. (It is this heritage of begging that people with disabilities are trying hard to shed: We no longer want to be called "handicapped" because the word derives from the practice of holding out one's cap in his hand when begging for alms.)

While Margaret certainly had much against her, she also had a great deal working for her. As we have already seen, she had an innate intelligence that helped her cope with her various disabilities. Her warm, loving nature tended to draw people toward her. But her greatest asset in coping with life on the streets was the profound depth of her relationship with God.

After the shock of realizing that there had been no mistake—that her parents had abandoned her to the streets of a town she did not know—Margaret, as other mystics before and after have done, recognized the spiritual gold in the human hardship of her life. She had been well schooled in the Gospels by Padre Capellano and no doubt recognized the opportunity to model the suffering in her life on the life and suffering of Jesus. This recognition was most likely underscored when, only hours after being abandoned by her parents, another homeless woman invited Margaret to spend her first night on the streets sleeping in a stable. The parallel is obvious.

*Life in the Cloister*

As so often happens with people whom societies marginalize, they come together to help one another. Margaret's remarkable grace in the midst of harrowing life circumstances, plus her obvious spiritual gifts and loving nature, began to draw people both like and unlike herself near to her. A consensus grew among them that Margaret should enter the local convent, ironically named the Convent of St. Margaret. There she would be able to live her spiritual life and be safe from the vagaries and hazards of life on the streets.

Margaret's disabilities had become well known in Castello, and the nuns at the convent were well aware of her physical situation. They accepted her with the mistaken impression that they would have to care for her. But Margaret was quite independent in caring for her personal needs, and she learned the corridors and corners of the convent as quickly as she had those of her parents' castle.

This seemingly flawless plan did not work out for Margaret. The nuns of St. Margaret's cloister had fallen from a strict observance of their Rule, ignoring night silence and entertaining frivolous visitors in the parlor. Margaret understood the requirements of the Rule and its goal: providing an atmosphere that would safeguard the spiritual lives of the nuns. She not only welcomed this but thrived on it, even after being confronted point-blank by the superior, who asked her to join the other sisters in their more relaxed approach to cloistered life.

Margaret's insistence on observing the original Rule created tension. One wonders if the tension was exacerbated by Margaret's disability. Many nondisabled people generally have (perhaps unconscious) expectations of how persons with disabilities should act: humble, grateful, willing to go along with the decisions others make for them. Disabled individuals, in the fourteenth century as well as in the twenty-first, often were not and are not expected to have a voice or to be at all assertive. Margaret's obedience to the original Rule, after the nuns had overlooked her disabilities and taken her in, was a tacit rebuke to them that they were not living the religious life they had vowed. The superior asked Margaret to leave.

Once again Margaret of Castello experienced extreme rejection. It must have cut into her soul to be cast out again on the streets, this time not because of her disabilities but because of her convictions. Was she tempted to give up, to despair, to turn against God? If so, her despair probably did not last long. Steeped in the Gospels, Margaret was acutely aware that suffering, especially the suffering of rejection, was experienced by Christ. And she had decided long ago to take up her cross to follow him.

### The Mantellate

Demonstrating heroic and charitable restraint, Margaret never told why the nuns had asked her to leave their cloister. Well-known in Castello, she remained homeless for only a short time. She joined the mantellate, the predecessor of today's Third Order Dominicans. (Fifty years later, another Italian saint, Catherine of Siena, also joined the mantellate.) Members of the mantellate wore a modified white Dominican habit, lived at home and dedicated their lives to serving God and practicing penance. They were addressed as "Sister" and were regarded with respect in Italian society.

Margaret took her lifestyle as a Third Order Dominican seriously. She became even more prayerful, reciting all 150 psalms and various offices daily. She rose at midnight to recite matins. In addition to the Divine Office, Margaret prayed in a deeper, more contemplative manner.

Prayer is a cornerstone of the Christian life. Authentic prayer invites us beyond a "God and me" mentality; it draws us to serve others. Margaret thus began a new ministry: She committed herself to visiting people in the city who were ill or dying. This small woman making her way through the streets at all hours of the day and night became a common sight in Castello.

Margaret would soon stop living on the streets, and for the rest of her life, she lived with some of the wealthiest families of Castello.

### Wondrous Works

According to Margaret's medieval biographer, one of her sister mantellates was afflicted with a tumor of the eye that was slowly robbing her of sight. The woman asked Margaret to pray for her, and her eye was completely healed.

Margaret's next mediation of divine power occurred when the home of the Venturinos, the family with whom she was living, caught on fire. In medieval times wealthy families heated their homes by building huge fires in the middle of their great rooms. Obviously, this practice was treacherous, sometimes burning down not only the family's home but also their neighbors'. One day the Venturinos' house caught fire with Margaret trapped alone inside. Neighbors had to restrain Lady Venturino from racing back into the burning building to rescue Margaret. However, they looked up to see Margaret calmly standing at the top of the staircase. She ignored pleas to flee and instead removed her Dominican mantle and threw it on the fire, which immediately went out.

Through these and other instances of mediating divine power, Margaret became quite famous in Castello and its surrounding areas.

Despite her growing fame, Margaret herself remained prayerful and humble, even as she embarked on her final ministry: visiting prisoners.

## Prison Ministry

Medieval prisons were brutal and inhumane. Prisoners were shackled, ill-fed and sometimes kept underground. Prison wardens readily accepted bribes to provide well-off prisoners with food while ignoring the poorer prisoners. Sanitary conditions were abominable, allowing diseases to spread rapidly. Margaret, accompanied by some of her sister mantellates, visited the prison often, bringing food, blankets and other necessities, as well as spiritual comfort. She also used her relationship with the nobility of Castello to bring about some improvements in the prison conditions.

## Margaret's Death and Burial

In 1320 Margaret, now thirty-three years old, was growing frail. By Easter of that year, her friends suspected that she would not live much longer. They were correct. Margaret of Castello, after receiving Eucharist and the last rites of the Catholic church, died on April 13, 1320, surrounded by Dominican friars as well as her sisters of the mantellate. Her death was peaceful; her burial was anything but.

In a warm climate like Italy's, dead bodies must be buried almost immediately. Her mantellate sisters washed her body and wrapped it in her in a black Dominican *mantilla* (cloak). Embalming was expensive, and therefore only used by the wealthy. The Dominican rule required poverty in death as well as life, so Margaret was not buried in a coffin.

As we have seen, Margaret was extremely popular in Castello. When word went out that she had died, scores of Castellans joined her funeral procession. Dominican friars and mantellates led her funeral cortege to the cemetery attached to Chiesa della Carita, the Dominican church, as Margaret had requested. However, when the townspeople perceived that their Margaret was to be buried in the cemetery, they raised an uproar, demanding that her body be placed in the church. The Dominican prior objected, but to no avail.

Then something amazing happened.

A couple with a young daughter who also had been born with multiple disabilities—unable to neither walk nor speak—placed their daughter's body next to Margaret's corpse and begged her intercession with God for healing. According to accounts, Margaret's left arm rose to touch the little girl. The child then rose to her feet and ran through the church, calling out in joy. Margaret of Castello's first miracle had taken place within hours of her death.

This ended the confrontation. Margaret was buried inside the church.

### Margaret's Beatification

Well aware that they were quite possibly dealing with a future saint, both church and civic officials in Castello were careful to investigate and document closely any claims of divine intervention through Margaret. They also embalmed her body. Embalming practices in medieval times differed greatly from those of today—internal organs were removed and replaced with fragrant herbs and spices. The longest a body could remain preserved was about two weeks; today's modern chemicals preserve a body for approximately twelve years. Margaret's body—except for some discoloration of the skin—remains uncorrupted today. It is on display at the School for the Blind in Castello. The church has traditionally viewed the lack of decay of a body as a sign of divine intervention. This along with any miraculous cures is serious consideration for sainthood.

Margaret's fame as an intercessor grew, with people from all over central Italy coming to her tomb to pray. Over two hundred affidavits are available testifying to miraculous cures of people with various conditions. Pope Paul V beatified her in 1609.

### The Disability Saint

Had there been amniocentesis in the 1300s, there probably never would have been a Margaret of Castello. Her parents' reaction to a child with multiple disabilities—to the point of abandoning her—is horrifying. However, as the fate of Baby M clearly shows, modern attitudes and practices toward babies born with disabilities can still be barbaric. As cruel as Margaret's parents were, at least they allowed her to live, rather than following the practice of exposing a "defective" child to the elements or tossing the child from a cliff as was done in Margaret's time.

Certainly, Margaret could easily be the "poster saint" for the anti-abortion movement, as well as for the thousands of homeless people who populate the streets of the world's wealthiest nation. But Margaret has a special place in the hearts of persons with disabilities. Six centuries before there was a disability rights movement, Margaret of Castello was demonstrating that one could indeed live a happy, productive and spiritual life even with many disabilities. Her strength came from God.

Although she could leave behind no writings because of her circumstances, her profound holiness touched every person she encountered. The fact that reverence for Margaret continues to this day in Castello indicates that her genuine holiness was for Castellans a roadmap to God.

*Margaret as Companion*

For a person with any level of disability, but especially one with severe or multiple disabilities, Margaret is an ideal companion. When feeling left out of something because of lack of transportation, a mountain of stairs or friends who find it inconvenient to let you join the fun, turn to Margaret. She lived it too. She knew well the feeling of being shunted aside. When you are tempted to wallow in self-pity because of your limitations, have a chat with the Disability Saint. Although she must have felt sorry for herself at times, with the help of grace she always seemed able to overcome her feelings and go on.

When dealing with any challenging aspect of life, ask Margaret of Castello for her intercession. Margaret "walked the walk" of a woman with many disabilities and also changed others' attitudes. She lived life on her own terms and transformed her daily challenges into spiritual opportunities full of grace. And she did it without vocational rehabilitation, computer technology or disability payments. She is a medieval role model for those of us with disabilities today. Her secret for coping—profound, unremitting love of God—is available to anyone.

Occasionally, humanity is gifted with individuals who are so clearly in love with God that their lives are like keyholes through which we glimpse divinity: Francis of Assisi, Teresa of Avila, Oscar Romero come to mind. There is little doubt that Margaret of Castello is in this company.

*Every* human life is God's creation. Each person, no matter how frail, disabled or physically weak, is vitally important to our God. It is precisely because every person reflects the image of God that we are called to do whatever is in our power not only to alleviate homelessness, poverty and abortion, but also to tear down the societal barriers that isolate persons with disabilities. And for those of us who live with disabilities, we can be proud to have as a role model Margaret, a woman with multiple disabilities whose simple holiness drew so many to God.

Margaret of Castello, a woman blind and of short stature, continues to cast a long shadow in the communion of saints. And those of us who live with disabilities of any sort can be proud to journey in her shadow.

## two

JULIAN OF NORWICH
*Our Companion in Serious Illness*
(1342–1413)

ady Julian of Norwich. First English woman of letters.
Rediscovered mystic. Renowned spiritual director of her time. Famed
for optimism in the midst of the darkness of the fourteenth century.
A marvelous spiritual companion for anyone coping with serious ill
ness or disability.

Even though we know little about her life, Julian of Norwich's
*Revelations of Divine Love,* written in 1373 and still quite popular today, is
a spiritual classic that recounts the visions of Jesus Christ granted to
Julian while she was close to death. It ranks as a spiritual classic for
many reasons, but is particularly important to those of us with disabilities or illnesses because of its themes of sickness as purification, its
constant reminder of God's profound love for us, and its famed
emphasis on optimism: "All shall be well."

Biographical details about Julian's life are sketchy. She was most
likely born in 1342, was perhaps a Benedictine nun before becoming

an anchorite and, despite her claim to being a "simple unlettered creature," was obviously familiar with Scripture and contemporary theological thinking. We do know one critically important date in her
life—May 8, 1373, the day on which she received sixteen successive
revelations (or "showings," as she called them) while deathly ill.

Some years before receiving these "showings," Julian had asked
for three gifts from God: (1) to understand Christ's Passion, (2) to be
ill to the point of death, and (3) to have three wounds from God: true
contrition, genuine compassion and sincere longing for God.

For anyone today who deals with the physical pain and emotional
struggles of serious illness, it is amazing to think that someone could
actually *pray* to God to be sickened to the point of death. Julian, however, is quite specific about her request: "[I] freely desiring that sickness [to be] so hard as to death, that I might in that sickness receive
all my rites of Holy Church, myself thinking that I should die, and
that all creatures might suppose the same that saw me: for I would
have no manner of comfort of earthly life."[1] She then tells why she
makes this mind-boggling prayer: "And this I meant for [that] I would
be purged, by the mercy of God, and afterward live more to the worship of God because of that sickness."[2] Julian asked to be spared nothing of the suffering of the fear, grief and pain that accompany the
dying process. "In this sickness I desired to have all manner of pains
bodily and ghostly that I should have if I should die, (with all the
dreads and tempests of the fiends) except the out-passing of the
soul."[3] She did add a caveat: "if it be Thy will that I have it."[4]

Incredible! Even given the medieval emphasis on asceticism and
the fact that as an anchoress Julian's whole life was dedicated to God,
to actually *ask* God for a terminal illness is simply stunning to us today.
What possible motivation could someone, even a devoted anchoress
of the fourteenth century, have for making such a bizarre request?
What did she need to be "purified" from that she would ask the God
who loved her to put her so close to death? To ask to be so ill that not

only she, but all those around her, would also believe that she was dying? Most of all, how can this wonderful fourteenth-century woman mystic be a companion to us today and teach us about suffering, illness and love?

Before we explore these questions, let us look at the life of Julian and how her beautiful, mystical classic *Revelations of Divine Love* came into being.

*Background*

Norwich, a port city in southeast England, was a bustling center of commerce and learning in Julian's day. Ships sailed to and from the continent, bringing merchandise, foreigners and, unfortunately, the germs that helped to spread the Black Death, or bubonic plague, that ravaged the fourteenth century. This century was a tumultuous time marked not only by the plague, but also by the Hundred Years War between England and France, frequent famines and the Great Schism, the period in the hierarchy of the Roman Catholic church when there were two competing claimants to the papacy. Julian's divinely inspired optimism of "All shall be well" is even more remarkable against the backdrop of this dark century.

*The Life of an Anchoress*

The life of an anchoress included not only spiritual direction of others, but many hours spent in prayer and solitude. Julian's "anchorhold" was a small room attached to the Church of St. Julian in Norwich. It had one small window into the church (the Anchoresses' Rule recommended that the day begin with a "visit" to the Blessed Sacrament every morning) and another small window through which food could be passed and spiritual advice sought and given. Often the anchoress had a "maiden," or servant, who tended to her needs of buying and preparing food, and generally kept the anchorhouse tidy. Also, cats were permitted to ward off the ubiquitous mice and rats of medieval times.

We know quite a bit about the anchoritic lifestyle because the *Ancrene Wisse (Anchoress' Guide)*, composed by an unknown author in the West Midlands of England, has come down through the centuries nearly intact. The *Ancrene Wisse* was both a practical and a spiritual guide, advising its charges on a plethora of topics ranging from dietary regulations ("Between meals you should not eat, snack, nibble fruit or anything"5) to clothing ("it does not matter if your clothes are white or black, so long as they are plain, warm and well-made"6). There is a long discussion about the etiquette of when to wear and when not to wear a wimple. Much counsel is given regarding the relationship between the anchoress and her "maiden," the author being quite clear that the spiritual life of the servant is decidedly the responsibility of her mistress: "[I]f they sin through your negligence, you will be called to account for it before the high judge."7 Therefore, "teach them earnestly to keep their rule, both for your sake and theirs—gently and lovingly, for so women's teaching ought to be."8 Despite the stern tone that pervades the *Ancrene Wisse*, the author takes care to allow for flexibility and individual need, advising the anchoresses in the end to follow the guide "according to your strength."9

Obviously, only someone profoundly in love with God could choose the rigorous lifestyle of an anchoress. The anchoritic lifestyle was a radical one, even for the fourteenth century: "The ceremony of enclosure...was for all practical purposes a kind of burial. Extreme unction was given, and the anchorite was literally sealed in, obliged under threat of excommunication to remain there until death."10 This certainly does not sound like an appealing lifestyle to us today. However, the anchoritic way of life did provide the space necessary for contemplative prayer, freeing the woman from living in the medieval households that were cramped, smoky and overflowing with people. Moreover, a woman who chose to be a "Martha" and marry and bear children worked from dawn until dusk in the ceaseless drudgery of running a medieval household. For the "Marys," those women with a deep propensity for contemplative prayer, the space and solitude that the anchorhold provided were perhaps a blessing. And, in Julian's case, this radical anchoritic lifestyle has given the world a mystic whose message is both profound and timeless.

## Suffering

One aspect of the life of an anchoress was the emphasis on Christ's Passion. The anchoress was called to be continually aware of Christ's suffering: from the moment she arose, she was to acknowledge the crucifix on the altar of her church. Each day the hour from noon to one was spent in special prayer in honor of Christ's last hour on earth. The many daily sufferings of the anchoress were continually viewed through the lens of the sufferings of Christ, with the goal of becoming more like him through identification with his Passion: "[n]ight and day you are up on God's cross,"[11] exhorted the *Ancrene Wisse*.

Although the austerity of the life of an anchoress may hold little appeal for contemporary women or men, the wisdom that anchoresses have passed down through the centuries can be invaluable to anyone searching for spiritual meaning in illness, disability or suffering of any type. Our contemporary culture tends to reject and fear suffering, thereby rejecting and fearing the people who experience it. This cultural bias can often make it terribly difficult to accept that the pain of one's life—whether loss, addiction or physical or mental illness—not only has meaning, but is also a continual invitation to grow closer in union with the crucified Jesus.

## Julian's Sickness

Against this background, it is somewhat easier to understand Julian of Norwich's plea to God to contract a terminal illness if it be the divine will: "And when I was thirty years old and a half, God sent me a bodily sickness, in which I lay three days and three nights; and on the fourth night I took all my rites of Holy Church, and weened not to have lived till day."[12] The deathly illness continued for three more days, with Julian and those attending her believing several times that she had died. As she lay apparently dying, Julian began to lament the fact of her imminent demise and wished to live longer, but only for one reason: "But it was to have lived that I might have loved God better, and longer time."[13] As always, Julian's heart was set on what God wanted first: "And I understood by my reason and by my feeling of my pains that I should die; and I assented fully with all the will of my heart to be at God's will."[14] God had granted her request: a terminal illness with its accompanying physical, emotional and spiritual agonies.

After assuring God that all she truly sought was the divine will, Julian began to experience paralysis in her lower body: "my body was dead from the middle downwards, as to my feeling."[15] She asked to be set upright in her bed with her head tilted toward heaven, "thinking on God while my life would last."[16]

A curate was sent for to administer the last rites. The priest placed a crucifix before Julian and bade her to look upon the image of her Savior. Though she thought that her heavenward gaze was sufficient remembrance of God at her dying moment, Julian, ever the obedient daughter of the church, "assented to set my eyes on the face of the Crucifix."[17] As she did so, she began to lose her vision—all she could perceive was darkness—with one exception: the image of the crucifix.

Next her upper body weakened, making her breathing heavy and labored. It was at this point that Julian believed herself clinically dead. It was also precisely at this exact time that she revived: "And in this [moment] suddenly all my pain was taken from me, and I was as whole (and specially in the upper part of my body) as ever I was afore."[18]

Julian was convinced that her miraculous recovery was from God: "I marveled at this sudden change; for methought it was a privy working of God, and not of nature."[19] She then recalled her earlier prayer, in which she had prayed that she would be granted both physical and mental experience of the Passion of Christ. Why? Quite simply because "I desired to suffer with Him."[20]

Immediately after making this appeal to God, the first of the sixteen revelations began. Not surprisingly, after the prayer request she had just uttered, the very first "showing" is of Christ's head surrounded by the crown of thorns: "In this [moment] suddenly I saw the red blood trickle down from under the Garland hot and freshly and right plenteously."[21]

Julian of Norwich's singularly privileged mystical journey had begun.

*The Showings*

Throughout the remainder of that day and night, Julian was granted a series of sixteen exceedingly vivid mystical visions involving Christ, Mary, the Trinity and God as both Father and Mother. Her mystical experience, she tells us, started at four in the morning and continued for almost twenty-four hours. Realizing the importance of her "showings," she wrote them down—twice. She wrote the first version, known as the Short Text, soon after her mystical experience. Over the next twenty years, she continued to meditate upon their significance, writing a fuller version, the Long Text, which more fully explicates their meaning. Using beautifully simple Old English imagery (God as our "Maker, Keeper, Lover," for example), Julian felt called to share the depth and significance of her showings with her "even-Christians," her touchingly egalitarian term for her fellow believers.

Did Julian of Norwich ever doubt if her showings were genuinely from God? It required tremendous courage for Julian, living in an age when women's voices were rarely heard, to trust that her message was indeed divinely inspired and to articulate it for the people of her time and all time.

As we have seen, *Revelations of Divine Love* sprang from Julian's sincere request of God to experience an illness that would make her deathly ill. We have already noted her reason for doing so—to be thoroughly cleansed of *anything* that would keep her from union with her Lord.

Why, though, would an anchoress ask for purification? Would not living the austere life dictated by the *Ancrene Wisse* be enough to purify one? The crux of Julian's desire is not so much what Julian wanted to *remove* from herself as what she wanted to gain for herself. To Julian, living according to "the worship of God" meant removing everything in her spiritual life that was an obstacle to her relationship with God. She wanted no subtle spiritual blocks, no interior obstacles, between herself and God. While it can be difficult for us to imagine any sinful tendencies in such a holy woman, most of the great mystics became more acutely aware of their personal failings as they drew closer to union with God.

We can only speculate as to the nature of what Julian felt she should be cleansed of and stand in awe that the depth of her desire for union with Jesus was so intense that she asked to be ill in order to achieve that union. For those of us already experiencing long-term illness, Julian sets an example. We too can allow our illnesses, albeit not requested, to serve as purifying elements in our spiritual lives. Whether one is experiencing the physical pain of chronic illness, the stigma of mental illness or the angst of terminal disease, Julian has demonstrated the way to spiritual wholeness. Like her, we can ask to be purified, to "live more according to the worship of God," confident that while we may not receive "showings," we *will* receive an abundance of strengthening grace.

How then does suffering purify us, cleanse us? Perhaps there is no greater teacher in life than suffering. Disability professionals have a simple slogan that says it well: "Bitter or better." Of course, those of us with disabilities must be open to the grace inherent in experiences of illness and disability. We must be able to trust, to hold onto God's hand during the most harrowing of life's experiences, be it severe pain, physical or emotional trauma or the dying process. God is there whether we are aware of the divine presence or not: "I am with you always, to the end of the age" (Matthew 28:20). In my personal experience, pain has a way of sanctifying, of making every moment sacred because it blocks out everything except God. When we allow it, pain can teach us the value of tiny things—the delightful taste of cold water, the voice of a loved one, the face of a friend. And since we "see from where we stand," almost every person who has lived with great pain or serious illness becomes more compassionate toward others who are not well. Suffering is often the purifying kiln which reshapes and remolds our hearts. It has the potential to teach us what is truly important in life: not necessarily climbing the corporate ladder or having a pristine house or a new car every year. These pale in comparison to the love of family and friends and the sacredness of our relationship with God.

*Uniting Our Passion*

It is certainly not a coincidence that Julian's first showing was the head of Jesus surrounded by the crown of thorns. As we have seen, a central focus of the anchoritic lifestyle was identification with Christ's Passion. Julian's goal, to grow daily closer to Christ by emulating his suffering, can be incorporated into the contemporary suffering person's spiritual life through many of the same methods the ancient anchoresses used.

By looking at a crucifix upon rising, choosing a certain amount of time each day to dedicate to praying with the Passion and inviting Jesus into the hardships of our own particular condition every day, we will grow ever closer in union with Christ. For example, the night before undergoing major surgery is a good time to pray with Jesus in his agony in the Garden of Gethsemane. When experiencing severe pain, think of the nails being driven into Jesus' hands and feet or how he felt hanging on the cross. If feeling down about the anguish your condition causes your loved ones, look at Jesus as he met his mother on the Via Dolorosa and share with him your feelings.

Most of all, uniting one's pain with that of Jesus on the cross not only sanctifies the pain but joins him in the wonderful act of redeeming the sin of the world. The old practice of "offering it up" can make one's suffering meaningful. A friend of mine has spinal stenosis disorder, a painful condition. She makes it a practice to offer every hour for a specific intention, thus offering to others the greatest gift she has to give: her suffering. It is vitally important, however, to acknowledge rather than deny the pain of one's own life and to consciously and continually give it over to God in whatever way seems best.

Occasionally one can be tempted to believe that it is presumptuous to attempt to identify with the sacred suffering of Jesus Christ. Jesus himself, however, invites his followers to do precisely that when he says, "If any want to become my followers, let them deny themselves and take up their cross daily and follow me" (Luke 9:23). Saint Paul invites Christians "by the mercies of God, to present your bodies as a living sacrifice, holy and acceptable to God" (Romans 12:1). When Julian says, "I desired to suffer with him," she invites her "even-Christians" of her day *and* ours to follow her example and unite again and again their suffering with that of Christ's, making their pain both meaningful and sacred.

### Mutuality of Suffering

We have seen that Julian's love for Christ is so profound that she desires to experience exactly what her Savior experienced, to physically feel what he physically felt. The key word in the sentence, the "pearl of great price" for those who desire to sanctify their own suffering, is the word *with*. A simple little word with a profound meaning: For the concept of mutuality implied in "with" means that not only do *we* suffer with Jesus, but *he suffers with us*. Julian invites us to suffer with our Savior, who in turn accompanies us in every step of our lives and is as close to us as our very breath.

Julian describes this divine-human intimacy in elegantly simple Old English: "For as the body is clad in the cloth, and the flesh in the skin, and the bones in the flesh, and the heart in the whole, so are we, soul and body, clad in the Goodness of God and enclosed. Yea, and more homely: for all these may waste and wear away, but the Goodness of God is ever whole."[22] In our contemporary culture, which glorifies self-sufficiency and autonomy, it can be challenging to believe that God is this close to us, that God loves us so dearly. Julian, however, in describing God's relationship with us as "homely," a word in the thirteenth century that meant deeply intimate, assures us that God's intimate, loving accompaniment is very real. God, our constant Lover, invites us to "cleave," or cling, to God as firmly as God clings to us. Julian asks us not only to be aware of this ever-present love but also to recognize that the pain in our lives is not only like Christ's pain; it is a conduit into his suffering, and hence into his love.

So whether one is lying on a gurney waiting to be wheeled into an operating room, living the chaos of bipolar disease, coping with a life-threatening illness such as cancer or AIDS, or dealing with human suffering of any kind, the invitation is the same: to be aware of God's loving presence, to *know* in one's heart, head and bones that God is always present, watching, loving, consoling us.

### "And All Shall Be Well"

Besides assuring us of God's ever-constant presence, Julian of Norwich also gives a tremendous gift to people who live with illness: the gift of *hope*. That a mystic could articulate such a firm message of joy-filled optimism in the midst of an era of suffering filled with war, plague and starvation is simply astonishing. Despite her life as an anchorite, Julian was not shielded from the hardships of her day because many of her contemporaries came to her for spiritual direction. She felt the heartache of grief, the pangs of hunger and the deprivations of war along with them. Yet because of her "showings" Julian had a secret that she wanted to share with her world and ours: *No matter what our earthly sufferings, all shall be well.* Indeed, Jesus impressed the message upon Julian by repeating it to her three times: *"but all shall be well, and all shall be well, and all manner of thing shall be well."*[23]

Well? How can things be well in the midst of plague and famine? Or in our day of AIDS, terrorism and thousands of people dying each day from starvation? The divine message seems to be that our earthly trials are minimal compared to our time in eternity with God. As Saint Paul writes, "What no eye has seen, nor ear heard, / nor the human heart conceived, / what God has prepared for those who love him" (1 Corinthians 2:9). This is the crux of living with suffering. It is crucial to hold onto this divine hope when we encounter great suffering. One suggestion is to repeat Julian's words as a prayer mantra: "All shall be well." We must beg God for the grace to know this with our heads and to live it with our hearts. For living with the hope of eternity will lead us to a life stance that, despite the limitations and other hardships of illness, will be centered on genuine joy. And joy—real, deep-down, God-infused joy—is a gift. A gift not just for ourselves, but for others. Few things baffle people as much as the witness of those of us who are ill or disabled and who also radiate the joy and optimism that can come only from God.

Julian of Norwich, author, anchoress, spiritual director, mystic of the fourteenth century, lived the very same God-infused joy and optimism every day. We in the twenty-first century can rejoice that Julian of Norwich let us in on her holy secret—ultimately, no matter what, "All shall be well."

## three

*I*t happens millions of times every day, in every part of the world: people performing tasks, large and small, for one another. No matter how small or large the act, loving one another is an essential part of the message Jesus handed on to his followers: "This is my commandment, that you love one another as I have loved you" (John 15:12). While popular music, movies and TV shows generally focus exclusively on romantic love, the love that Jesus spoke of is a broad, giving-of-self love: the same self-emptying, self-giving love that Jesus lived and for which he died. Self-giving love is more about our will, our choosing to follow a course of action, than about our feelings and emotions; it means showing up, being there in need and reaching out to and caring about one another.

Being a caregiver by providing assistance, whether physical, emotional, spiritual or financial to another person is the very essence of the self-giving love of Jesus Christ. And most of the people who carry out this special mission today are women: "Women provide the majority of informal care to spouses, parents, parents-in-law, friends and neighbors, and they play many roles while caregiving—hands-on health provider, care manager, friend, companion, surrogate decision-maker and advocate."[1] Measured monetarily, the care that women provide is invaluable: "In fact, the value of the informal care that women provide ranges from $148 billion to $188 billion annually."[2] Certainly, there are many men who are caregivers, but the bulk of caregiving comes from women.

Sometimes the mission of being a caregiver can be demanding, as when the person one is caring for has Alzheimer's disease or a severe physical disability. It can be helpful to caregivers to recall that they are literally being the hands and feet of the Lord, that they are performing tasks that he would perform if he were physically present. The prayer of Saint Teresa of Avila puts it well: "Christ has no body now but yours, no hands, no feet but yours."[3] Jesus loves each person unconditionally and wants all to be cared for when care is needed. Because he is not physically present, he needs people to carry out his special mission. How wonderful it is to be carrying out Jesus' own mission!

*Catherine of Genoa*

Fortunately, caregivers have a role model and friend they can turn to for spiritual companionship among the communion of saints: Saint Catherine of Genoa, a married, full-time-working woman who knew well the rewards and demands of caregiving. And, contrary to what one might expect, she did not always find her caregiving role an easy one. As we will see, she did it entirely for love—a deep, passionate love for Jesus.

Catherine of Genoa is revered to this day by the citizens of her native city for her heroic devotion and service to its poor people, especially during the plague of 1493. She is also highly regarded by the Catholic church for her spiritual works *Purgation and Purgatory, The*

*Spiritual Dialogue* and her *Life*. Although Catherine did not actually compose these herself (she didn't have the time), they were written by close associates and are deemed by the church to be her authentic voice.

### Heritage

Catherine was born into the Fieschi family of the northern Italian seaport city of Genoa in 1447. The Fieschis, one of Genoa's wealthiest and most illustrious families, were prominent in both church and state: Two popes, Innocent IV and Adrian V, were Fieschis, and Catherine's father, Jacopo, served as the viceroy of Naples. Like many female saints, Catherine was a quiet and devout child, renowned for her beauty. At the age of thirteen, Catherine wanted to follow her sister into an Augustinian convent but was refused because she was too young. A year later her father died and, as was customary, her older brother became her guardian. Her brother decided to marry her off to Giuliano Adorno, a member of another aristocratic Genovese family.

### Marriage

Giuliano may have been an aristocrat, but he was certainly not a gentleman. In *Enduring Grace: Living Portraits of Seven Women Mystics,* Carol Lee Flinders describes Catherine's husband Giuliano: "Profligate and irascible at once, he is said to have had a singularly weak character."[4] More importantly, his carousing, gambling and womanizing lifestyle was precisely the opposite of his young wife's. Giuliano eventually had an illegitimate child with his mistress. Obviously, with Catherine's spiritual inclinations and great love of God, their marriage was doomed from the start.

The *Catholic Encyclopedia* describes the marriage: "Details are scanty, but it seems at least clear that Catherine spent the first five years of her marriage in silent, melancholy submission to her husband; and that she then, for another five, turned a little to the world for consolation in her troubles."[5] Psychologists today would perhaps describe her "silent, melancholy submission" as deep depression, a response to her husband's behavior and neglect. Perhaps to distract herself from her marital woes, Catherine devoted the next five years to participating in the life of Genovese society, but its frivolous nature could not appease her hunger for deeper meaning in life, and she again plunged into depression.

*Turning Point*

Catherine's family was deeply concerned about her emotional state. On March 22, 1473, in an attempt to ease Catherine's depression, her sister, an Augustinian nun, invited her to speak with her own confessor. Catherine never did make the confession because the priest was called away. However, "[s]he had hardly knelt down before him when her heart was suddenly pierced by an immense love of God, with such a clear awareness of her own miseries and sins and of God's goodness, that she was ready to swoon."[6]

This profound experience of God changed Catherine of Genoa's life on many levels. The smoldering embers remaining from her childhood love for God were now fanned into a passionate, blazing fire: "From the moment of that sudden vision of herself and God, the saint's interior state seems never to have changed, save by varying in intensity."[7]

Catherine's deep religious experience was the touchstone of her spiritual life. From that moment on she lived in continual contact with God. Energized by this experience, she shook off her depressed state and started going into the slums of Genoa to minister with the people there. The infused love of God that she received transformed her life. "She would carry that vision before her mind's eye always, and it would hurl her into a life of heroic service—to Christ living in the tormented shapes of thousands upon thousands of suffering men, women, and children."[8]

Catherine of Genoa's religious experience and resulting ministry to people who were ill and indigent perfectly illustrate the commandment to love your neighbor as yourself. Catherine's *Spiritual Dialogue*, a conversation between her weaker self (Human Frailty) and God (the Spirit), describes her explicit call: "God said to her, you will work for a living. You will be asked to do works of charity among the poor sick, and when asked you will clean filthy things.... If I find that you consider some things repugnant I will have you so concentrate on them that they will no longer be such."⁹ What a mission! God is asking Catherine not only to minister among the poorest of the poor, those not able to care for themselves at all, but also to overcome any repugnance she might have for any of her caregiving duties. By dealing with her aversion to certain necessary tasks, God asks Catherine to become stronger and overcome her natural inclinations, which is precisely what she eventually did.

The *Spiritual Dialogue* continues: "And with that, one day the women in a confraternity of mercy asked Catherine for assistance, and she answered the call. She found many who were horribly sick, full of lice and foul-smelling. Some of them, because of the intensity of their suffering, were desperate. Entering the place was like entering a tomb; but Catherine was determined to minister to the sick and give them some consolation, even those who cursed anyone who came to help them."¹⁰ Surely her first visits must have been extremely difficult for a lady of society like herself, someone who was accustomed to having servants handle the basic chores necessary to run a household. Now Catherine herself was asked to enter establishments that were tomb-like, filthy and occupied by people who were desperately ill. On top of all this, it is clear that some people not only rejected her ministrations, but even cursed her for coming.

Her difficulties continued: "It seemed that the Spirit in these most trying tasks was having her experience utter wretchedness. Her Human Frailty was besieged on two sides—first, it found that wretchedness repugnant; and in addition it was suffering a terrible solitude, since the Spirit was so occupied with inner dialogue that it was cut off from external things."[11] Why would the God who so clearly loved her ask this woman to experience "utter wretchedness" and keep her so preoccupied with her inner dialogue that she was "cut off from external things"? Perhaps the answer is that God's wisdom is far beyond our human comprehension. God knows each individual's capacity and of what each of us is capable. What God asked of Catherine was indeed very difficult, but at the same time she received and accepted the grace necessary to perform it.

### Lice

Catherine soon began to deal with a new challenge: lice. "Now to assure the annihilation of her Human Frailty, since dealing with lice made Catherine almost vomit, the Spirit said: 'Take a handful of them, put them in your mouth and swallow them. That way you will free yourself of your nausea.' She shuddered but did as she was told, learning to handle them as if they were pearls."[12] This was as offensive to Catherine of Genoa in the fourteenth century as it is to us today. Although the request seems extreme, it does offer wisdom. Forcing ourselves to do something that we personally find repugnant can, as with Catherine, help us to overcome our aversion. We must remember, too, that God challenges us like this to help us grow. Had Catherine given in to her horror of lice, she would never have been able to continue with her vitally needed ministry.

### Giuliano

While Catherine was learning how to cope in her new role as caregiver, her husband Giuliano's lifestyle as a wastrel came to an end. After years of wasteful spending, Giuliano went bankrupt. He was forced to rent out the palatial home he shared with Catherine and move to a more modest one located near the Pammetone, a great hospital built specifically for the poor people of Genoa.

While the material cups of his life were now empty, his spiritual ones began to be filled. Giuliano's earthly bankruptcy became his spiritual salvation. Seeing the error of his ways, he began to live differently, eventually becoming a Third Order Franciscan. He also joined Catherine in ministering to the poor people of Genoa. In 1479 Catherine and Giuliano were invited to work at the Pammetone Hospital, where Catherine served in every capacity—from the most menial tasks at the hospital to eventually becoming its director in 1490.

In 1493 the plague struck Genoa, killing almost 80 percent of those citizens unable to escape to the countryside. Giuliano became gravely ill, and Catherine was unstinting in her care for him throughout the several months of his illness. He died that fall, leaving the remainder of his money to his wife "to provide the means for her continuing to lead her quiet, peaceful, and spiritual mode of life."[13]

*Calling on Jesus*

Because of her great love for Jesus, Catherine herself contracted the plague and almost died. She visited a dying woman who was a Third Order Franciscan and urged her to call on Jesus. "Unable to articulate, the woman would move her lips, and it was conjectured that she was calling Him as well as she could. When she saw the woman's mouth filled, as it were, with Jesus, Catherine could not restrain herself from kissing it with great and tender affection. As a result she, too, caught the plague and very nearly died of it."[14] Some actions of saints can be incomprehensible to us. Catherine's love for Jesus, her need for Jesus, overcame her natural instinct for self-preservation; she literally almost died from her desire for union with Jesus.

*Respite*

The remaining ten years of Catherine's life were quite different from her early and middle years. Her years of being steeped in God's love—and only God's love—came to a culmination with two beautiful gifts. The first was the gift of companionship in the form of a young businessperson named Ettore Vernazza, who, while helping her care for plague patients, was drawn to Catherine's spiritual depth and genuine holiness. He became her spiritual son and was changed for life by his friendship with the utter self-giving of Catherine of Genoa. He later founded the religious community known as the Oratory of Divine Love, as well as institutions for indigent people in several locations in Italy.

Catherine's second gift was one she never before had: a spiritual director. Don Catteneo Marabotto, who succeeded Catherine as director of the Pammetone, also became her confessor and spiritual director. While Catherine was delighted to have someone with whom she could share her profound spiritual journey, Father Marabotto was perhaps a bit intimidated by his task: "She never questioned that Father Marabotto was God's gift to her, and for his part, he knew himself to be nothing but a channel of grace, for he never knew what he was going to say to her until the moment arose."[15] Don Marabotto and Ettore Vernazza were responsible for composing Catherine's biography and other writings.

*The Death of Catherine*

Around the year 1508, Catherine's health was failing. She began to speak of her desire to die if it were to be God's will. The next year God bestowed on her the insight that her death would be drawn-out and painful, as so often happens with saints and mystics. (This will be evident again in the stories of Kateri Tekakwitha and Thérèse of Lisieux.) Perhaps this suffering is Jesus' final request of his beloved ones, with the invitation to unite their anguish to that of his on the cross. Or perhaps Jesus needs this final witness, this last self-giving, for the edification of those who watch.

Catherine says of her final illness: "It is hard to imagine what the Spirit had human weakness undergo—the suffering was so intense that those near her could barely endure the sight of that pain. Suffering broke that body from head to toe, so that there was no part of it that was not tormented by inner fire. There was also much internal bleeding."[16] The precise nature of Catherine's illness remains a mystery. The doctors who attended her were unable to diagnose it, let alone treat it. She could not eat or drink for lengthy periods, was unable to sleep at night and described herself as "burning within and without, and could not move of her own strength but had to be helped in all things."[17] The woman who devoted her entire life to self-giving love of others was now in need of care herself.

As word of her impending death spread, her followers and friends, as well as many others, gathered around her bed. She died in the early morning hours of Sunday, September 15, 1510. Fittingly, she was first buried near the chapel of the Pammetone Hospital. More than a year later her body was exhumed and found to be amazingly intact, much like Margaret of Castello two centuries earlier. She was then buried in a marble sepulchre inside the chapel, where her body remains largely uncorrupted and viewable to this day. Catherine of Genoa was canonized by Pope Clement XII on May 18, 1733.

*Caregiving*

For caregivers who find the responsibility of caring for another person challenging, it may be helpful to turn to Catherine of Genoa. She knew well that caregiving tests the depths of one's spirit, commitment and love, but she also knew the secret of providing loving care. She invites us to call on Jesus, to share with him our feelings, concerns, resentments and worries. She challenges us not only to *be* like Jesus, but to *see* Jesus in the person for whom we are providing care. She could even suggest a scriptural mantra: "Just as you did it to one of the least of these who are members of my family, you did it to me" (Matthew 25:40).

It may be surprising to some that a woman, even a woman who is a saint, could have struggles in nurturing and providing care for others. It is simply expected of women to perform these duties: "Of our care givers, and ourselves in care-giving roles, I think we expect, ideally at least, something resembling unconditional and unstinting love:

the compassion and tenderness, in short, of a mother, a perfect mother."[18] The reality, however, is that no human can provide this "unconditional and unstinting love" because it comes from one source only—God. Being the "perfect mother" certainly is an ideal, the ultimate in self-giving love, but it is an ideal that no human will ever meet—not even Catherine of Genoa.

Not long after Catherine had her conversion experience, she told God that she found it difficult to love her neighbor, because she could not love anyone other than God. "How then shall I act?" She asked God. "And she received this interior answer: 'Whoever loves me, loves all that I love.'"[19] She lived out this command of love in her ministry of caregiving. Since God made it clear to Catherine that divine love includes all people, she treated all, especially the people who were the most ill, with the utmost respect, recognizing each person's innate dignity.

Treating all with respect is a central tenet of Christ-based caregiving. When an adult is reduced to a childlike state due to illness or disability, it is sometimes tempting to forget the individual's God-given dignity and treat that person like a child. However, it is crucially important to avoid the patronizing tone of voice, the pats on the head or other subtle and not-so-subtle indications of pity or condescension. Even adults who experience severe cognitive loss due to dementia are still adults with life experience and should be treated as such. It may be helpful at such times to remember that Catherine of Genoa was respectful to all, even those who cursed her when she attempted to minister to them.

*On Hearing "Thank You"*

We all need to be needed. Even those who become frail due to aging or illness still need to know that they are needed, that they have some purpose in life. This need is even greater for those with a background in the helping professions. For one to be a giver all of her or his life and then reach the point of having to depend on another is extremely difficult. It can be helpful to the care-receiver's self-esteem to let her or him know that life still has meaning. In this vein, it is a good idea to empower the individual by asking him to perform tasks that he is able to do. For example, a family member who is unable to get out of bed can be asked to answer the phone during the day. Even individuals who are extremely frail can be asked to pray and offer their personal pain for a specific intention. And, of course, those individuals need to hear those two words that they say so often to others: "thank you." Again, we all have the very human need to be needed.

*Self-Care*

Self-giving does not mean self-negating. Knowing one's limits is particularly important for caregivers. The care and nurturing that caregivers give to others should also be directed toward themselves. Since we cannot give what we do not have, it is important for caregivers, especially full-time caregivers, to attend to their own needs, to be sure that their own physical, spiritual and emotional wells are replenished regularly. Throughout Catherine's years of ministry at the Pammetone Hospital, a small room was set aside for her to retire to in order to fulfill her need for deep communication with God. She was thus able to fulfill her primary need and continue her ministry refreshed.

*Care-Receivers*

Mutuality in the caregiving relationship is as important as in any other relationship; those of us who receive care from another person also have responsibilities in the relationship. We must learn to be clear and direct in communicating our needs, but not demanding. While we may not be physically able to give back to our caregivers, we *can* be emotionally supportive. In an interview shortly after her husband's death, Dana Reeve, wife of well-known actor Christopher Reeve, said of their relationship: "I demanded almost as much of our relationship after his disability as before—basically telling him: 'You need to be my husband. I am there to support you; and you need to support me.' I think it kept our relationship alive."[20]

It is also important to express gratitude frequently and not take caregivers, even paid caregivers, for granted. We present our caregivers with the opportunity to act as Jesus did toward us, just as we can be seen as the suffering Jesus to them. We need to remember, too, that being a care-receiver does not diminish our worth one iota in God's eyes, and it should not diminish our worth in our own. Certainly, this is not easy when one cannot perform simple tasks of everyday living.

Catherine of Genoa has a suggestion for those of us on the receiving end of care: "Whether I eat or drink, move or stand still, speak or keep silent, sleep or wake, see, hear or think; whether I am in church, at home or in the street, in bad health or good, dying or not dying, at every hour and moment of my life I wish all to be in God."[21] In other words, every single experience of our life can be grounded in God if we want it to be. We have only to continue to turn to God in whatever life situation, good day or bad day, hating our dependence or accepting it or just wishing circumstances were different: We can invite the God who loves us beyond measure into it all.

With the baby-boomer population aging, more people than ever will require assistance with activities of daily living: "Unpaid informal caregivers, primarily family members, neighbors and friends, currently provide the majority of long-term care services. Informal caregiving will likely continue to be the largest source of direct care as the baby boomer generation retires, with estimates of informal caregivers rising from 20 million in 2000 to 37 million in 2050, an increase of 85 percent."[22]

The handwriting is on the wall: Most of us will be on one side or the other of the care-based exchange of love. Fortunately, a woman who lived centuries ago has much to teach us about both giving and receiving care. She is more than willing to accompany us in whatever way we need her friendship. We can certainly trust her wisdom, knowing it comes from the One who told her: "Whoever loves me loves all that I love."

## four

SAINT IGNATIUS OF LOYOLA
*Our Companion in Temporary Disability*
(1491–1556)

*J*gnatius of Loyola. Many with only a cursory knowledge of the Catholic church know of him by name if not by reputation: founder of the Jesuits, author of the renowned *Spiritual Exercises*, great saint and mystic. Yet none of this—the tremendous and far-reaching influence of the Jesuits in education, the countless lives affected through the *Spiritual Exercises*, the incalculable influence of Ignatius on the church—may have happened had not the young Ignatius had his own taste of disability.

For Ignatius of Loyola, illness came in the form of a temporary disability from a battle wound and a long convalescence that forced him to stop and take a look at his life. And he did not like what he saw: a vain young man of idle pursuits. Since Ignatius dictated his *Autobiography* at the end of his life to one of his Jesuit brothers, we are fortunate to have his own account of his injury and the subsequent transformation of his life that flowed from it.

Ignatius himself attests to his rather shallow lifestyle in the first sentence of his *Autobiography:* "Until the age of twenty-six he was a man given over to vanities of the world; with a great and vain desire to win fame he delighted specially in the exercise of arms."[1] In keeping with Ignatian humility, Ignatius refers to himself in the third person. During the long months of Ignatius's disability, God gently and quietly offered him the greatest of gifts: the grace of conversion. Conversion comes in all shapes and sizes. Saul of Tarsus was knocked off his horse. Francis of Assisi was moved by the wounds of a man with leprosy. Ignatius of Loyola's conversion unfolded slowly, like the petals of a summer flower coming into full bloom. While Ignatius lay recovering from his leg injury, God entered into his disability and sowed the seeds of what would eventually flower into Ignatian spirituality. Conversion, however, is always a two-way street. God can only offer; *we* must respond. Respond Ignatius did, and the church and the world were forever changed.

## Background

Born in 1491, the future Saint Ignatius was the thirteenth and youngest child of a noble family in the Basque section of Spain. Ignatius's father, Beltrán Yañez de Loyola, was a military man who had fought against the Moors and was fiercely loyal to King Ferdinand and Queen Isabella. His mother, Marina Sáenz de Licona, a member of Castilian nobility, died shortly after his birth. Her infant son was placed with a village woman to nurse.

The world into which Ignatius was born was a turbulent and exciting one. The year after his birth saw Columbus, under the standard of Ferdinand and Isabella, discover the Americas. That same year the Moors were driven from Spain at the battle of Granada. Meanwhile the winds of the Protestant Reformation were starting to sweep through the Catholic church.

Ignatius's family was known for its military valor and its staunch Catholicism. It was a worldly Catholicism, however, one that allowed for a loose morality and a macho culture in which military prowess was prized above all else. The Loyolas were a proud, aristocratic family with a long military history.

As the youngest, Ignatius was steeped in these family values. He was a proud young man, almost as proud of his blond hair as he was of his skill with buckler and sword. As part of his education, he was sent to the Arevalo, home of Juan Valesquez de Cuellar, an old friend of his father and official at the royal court. This is where the young Ignatius became steeped in the ideals of chivalry and courtly love. He lived to the hilt the life of the romantic courtier, refining his abilities in fencing and courtly dancing, engaging earnestly in love and romance, and possessing rather loose morals. Polanco, a brother Jesuit of Ignatius and his earliest biographer, said of him: "Like all the young men who live at court and dream of military exploits, he was rather free in affairs of the heart, in games of chance, and in matters of honor."[2]

*Ignatius's Injury*
The dashing young Ignatius was fighting fiercely at the battle of Pamplona when a French cannonball smashed through the fortress wall and tore through the young knight's legs, shattering the right one and wounding the left. The battle was lost; Ignatius was captured by the French, who "treated the wounded man very well, with courtesy and kindness."[3] French doctors cared for his wounds and attempted to set the bones of his shattered right leg. Ignatius was then transported to his ancestral home of Loyola Castle. The journey was no doubt exceedingly painful, as he had to be carried on a litter in the open air through steep mountain passes and deep valleys.

After two weeks the caravan arrived at Loyola. Since Ignatius's father had died in 1507, his older brother, Martín García, was now lord of the castle. Martín was away fighting, but his wife, Magdalena de Araoz, a former lady-in-waiting to Queen Isabella, received her young brother-in-law and supervised his long convalescence.

Unfortunately, the shattered bones of the right leg, which had been set by the French doctors, had become unknit, probably due to the continually jarring nature of the journey. When the local physicians and surgeons examined the leg, they agreed it needed to be reset. Anyone who has experienced the trauma of surgery only to hear that it must be "redone" can imagine the young Ignatius's desolation as he heard the news that he must undergo the pain and trauma of a second surgery. He tells us: "This butchery was done again; during it, as in all the others he suffered before or since, he never spoke a word nor showed any sign of pain other than to clench his fists."[4] As this operation, like the first, took place several centuries before anesthesia, the physical pain was obviously excruciating.

Shortly after this operation, Ignatius's overall condition took a dramatic turn for the worse. He became so ill that the doctors began to despair for his life. While we do not know the precise physical reason for Ignatius's grave condition, it may well be that a serious infection set in after the surgery, as the importance of sterile conditions was not known at the time. Even today, with medical personnel taking every precaution possible in operating rooms, staph infections are not uncommon in hospitals.

In light of the fact that Ignatius's spirituality had not yet begun to mature, it is worth noting that he was still very much aware of his need for God's grace and the spiritual strength available through the sacraments. After being advised that he was possibly facing death, Ignatius went to confession. He, like most people of his day, was also keenly aware of the significance of the liturgical year: He noted that it was the Feast of John the Baptist; the next day marked the Vigil of Saints Peter and Paul. Saint Peter was one of Ignatius's favorites, as well as the patron of the entire house of Loyola. Just before midnight, as the vigil of Peter and Paul ended and the actual feast began, Ignatius experienced a remarkable recovery. The *Autobiography* states: "Our Lord willed that he should begin to improve that very midnight. His improvement proceeded so quickly that some days later it was decided that he was out of danger of death."[5]

The bones of Ignatius's leg started to knit together; however, they did not heal in a straight alignment. This resulted in a lump below the knee. Also, the right leg was now considerably shorter than the left, potentially leaving him with a pronounced limp. While many would no doubt consider these disabilities minor, the dashing young Ignatius could not accept them. His vanity would not tolerate the bony protuberance on the right leg: "because he was determined to follow the world and he thought that it would deform him."[6] The lump would be quite noticeable in the high-legged boots that fashionable young knights wore. In Ignatius's view, walking with an obvious limp would not only severely hamper his ability to engage in sword fights and dancing, but also make him less attractive to the noble ladies he desired. As he cherished above all his life as a knightly courtier, with its call to arms, its romancing of aristocratic ladies, its rugged, action-based lifestyle, he determined to do everything possible to remove both lump and limp.

*Cosmetic Surgery*

With this in mind, he pleaded with his doctors to do what they could to remove the bony lump and stretch his right leg to match the length of the left leg. His physicians were reluctant, in view of the fact that the bones had healed completely and that removing the lump would necessitate once more sawing through the skin and then sawing off the protuberance. Again, this would be done with no anesthesia, causing indescribable anguish for what was in effect cosmetic surgery: "They said that indeed it could be cut away, but that the pain would be greater that all those that he had suffered, because it was already healed and it would take some time to cut it. Yet he was determined to make himself a martyr to his own pleasure."[7]

No one in the Loyola household expected Ignatius to undergo this exceedingly painful procedure. Ignatius himself tells us that his older brother Martín, head of the castle, was horrified at the thought of it. No doubt the rest of his family also advised against it, not wanting to see their young brother suffer so excruciatingly. However, Ignatius was definitely a man of strong resolution and will. Once he had decided on a course of action, he went through with it.

*Self-Image*

The fact that the young Ignatius of Loyola requested to undergo again the acutely excruciating agony not only of surgery without anesthesia, but also surgery that required cutting through his flesh and then sawing off the bony lump, tells us much about him. First, this ordeal required great physical courage. While Ignatius had already demonstrated his capacity for bravery in the siege of Pamplona, his actually requesting this procedure with its physical agony is as puzzling to the modern reader as it was horrifying to Ignatius's family.

But maybe something deeper than mere vanity was going on in the psyche of this future saint. Perhaps his eagerness to remove the lumpy protuberance was Ignatius's desperate clinging to his former self.

As anyone who has experienced a serious physical trauma knows, dealing with the physical loss is only one part of the ordeal. The emotional aspects can be just as devastating. One's core identity can be shaken gravely. One of the major emotional adjustments for a person in the initial stages of physical disability is dealing with a changed body image. This is difficult for anyone. For someone like Ignatius, who viewed himself as a strong and capable person, any lessening of the ability to do what he had always done, any diminishment of physical function would be devastating emotionally. Understandably, the dashing young cavalier was not yet ready to live with even a minor disability, not willing to have his former lifestyle or his appearance altered in any way.

Ignatius's ordeal was not quite over. Removing the bony lump was not enough for him; he also demanded that his physicians do all they could to lengthen his right leg so that he would not limp: "After the flesh and excess bone were cut away, means were taken so the leg would not be so short; many ointments were applied to it, and, as it was stretched continually with instruments, he suffered martyrdom for many days."[8]

### Grieving

The *Autobiography* does not say much about Ignatius's emotional reactions to his disability and long period of recovery. Aside from his obvious distress over how the lump would spoil his appearance, he does not share his inner emotional reactions to his convalescence. It is not hard to imagine, however, that as he lay on his bed in his family home, his thoughts turned to how he used to stroll about the castle, ride his horse, and engage in swordplay. Did he ever feel angry or depressed? Did he bargain with God? While he does not share his inner feelings explicitly, it is certainly plausible that the young future saint struggled through all the typical phases of grieving, just as any person today with a similar loss must come to grips with it through the grieving process.

### Conversion

While knowledge of his emotions in his newly disabled state is scant, Ignatius's account of his spirituality is thorough. Spiritual directors have long been aware that grace builds on nature: God draws each person closer by working through that person's unique personality. This is especially true in conversion. As the Old Testament story of Elijah hiding in the cave illustrates, God speaks to human hearts sometimes in earthquakes, sometimes in fire, and sometimes in the soft whisper of the wind. In Ignatius's case, God worked through his love of reading and considerable gift of imagination. For his part, the young cavalier responded enthusiastically to the grace that God offered, not realizing he was becoming increasingly saintly.

While the doctors were busy attempting to restore Ignatius's leg, God's grace was slowly seeping into Ignatius's soul. In addition to his love of exploits with sword and shield, Ignatius was an avid reader, especially of the romantic novels popular in Spain in his day. Although his strength had returned, he still needed to remain in bed, and he asked for the romantic novels that he so enjoyed.

His sister-in-law Magdalena, however, was renowned for her religious devotion. A prayerful woman, she believed that romance novels were too worldly and did not permit them in the Loyola household. Thus she gave her young brother-in-law *The Life of Christ* by Ludolph Saxony, a German priest, and *The Golden Legend*, a book of lives of the saints. To pass the time, Ignatius read these religious books.

And then a remarkable thing happened: The worldly young knight began to enjoy what he was reading. He read and reread both books, becoming, as he says, "rather fond of what he found written there."[9] Not only did he read about Christ and the saints, but he also began to muse about their lives and exploits. Along with this spiritual fantasizing, however, he still engaged in idle imaginings about the noble woman whom he would like to serve and perhaps with whom he was even in love: "He imagined what he would do in the service of a certain lady, the means he would take so he could go to the country where she lived, the verses, the words he would say to her, the deeds of arms he would do in her service."[10] While we will never know for certain the identity of the "certain lady," speculation centers upon Princess Catherine, a beautiful young woman who was the sister of King Charles of Spain.

Ignatius's active imagination seesawed back and forth between rumination upon the noble deeds he would perform in the service of his lady and his desire to imitate, indeed surpass, the lives of the saints about whom he was reading. Then an even more remarkable thing happened: Ignatius, being rather introspective for all that he was so action-oriented, began to notice that his inner emotional state fluctuated according to what he fantasized about: "This succession of such diverse thoughts, either of the worldly deeds he wished to achieve or of the deeds of God that came to his imagination, lasted for a long time, and he always dwelt at length on the thought before him, until he tired of it and turned to other matters."[11]

As Ignatius's fantasies fluctuated between the noble deeds he would perform in the service of his lady and the heroic deeds he would perform in the service of God, he began to notice a difference. Imaginings about romantic exploits left his spirit dry and empty, whereas his imaginative deeds performed for God filled him with joy: "But when he thought of going to Jerusalem, barefoot and eating nothing but herbs and all undergoing the other rigors that he saw the saints had endured, not only was he consoled when he had these thoughts, but even after putting them aside, he remained content and happy."[12] Thus were planted the seedlings of what would eventually become the famed Ignatian method of discernment of spirits.

At this point in Ignatius's conversion, the action of God became more explicit. One evening, while falling asleep, Ignatius had a vision of the Virgin Mary: "From this sight he received for a considerable time very great consolation, and he was left with such loathing for his whole past life and especially for the things of the flesh, that it seemed that all the fantasies he had previously pictured in his mind were driven from it."[13] Since reviewing one's past life and repenting one's actions are signs of deepening conversion, it is clear that Ignatius's conversion was deepening profoundly through his continual response to the grace of God.

One hallmark of conversion is exhibiting deep regret for many things in our past lives. So it was with Ignatius: "From this reading he gained not a little insight, and he began to think more earnestly about his past life and about the great need he had to do penance for it."[14] Ignatius was not exaggerating the gravity of his past sins; we know that he had quite a wild youth. As we have already seen, despite the Catholicism of his family, the morality of the day was lax and so were Ignatius's personal values. Ignatius admitted that he had been quarrelsome and given to fighting and gambling.

As Ignatius lay convalescing, he had ample time to remember his past sins; however, he did not stay fixated on them but rather resolved to perform penance and move on. Again, God offered grace. It would have been easy for Ignatius to become stuck on his guilt and never grow spiritually. However, Ignatius chose not only to repent his past but also to reform his life and dedicate it to God.

By this time, Ignatius's oft-stated desire to perform penance and go on a pilgrimage to Jerusalem was not unrealistic, for his right leg was slowly healing and he was growing stronger. Also, his new outlook on life became apparent to his family: "His brother and the rest of the household knew from his exterior the change that had been working inwardly in his soul."[15] No doubt they were shocked to see their young brother, formerly so taken with things of the world, now speaking openly about things of God. His new ideals and goals, so radically different from his former ones, indicate the depth of his conversion. Authentic spirituality always propels one outward to speak of God, live for God, work for God.

*Remainder of His Life and Death*

Finally healed, Ignatius resolved to act immediately on his desire to embark on a pilgrimage to Jerusalem. Despite the protestations of his older brother, Ignatius left his home castle of Loyola in February of 1522. His ten-month convalescence was over; his life as a devout Christian had begun.

The beautiful flower of the young Ignatius's conversion had just started to bloom. God would deepen and refine it later, allowing Ignatius and the religious order he founded in 1540, the Society of Jesus, to perform great deeds in the service of Christ. Once fully healed, Ignatius threw himself into action for the Eternal King as fervently as he had thrown himself into action for his earthly one.

In the summer of 1556 Ignatius contracted a fever and died. He was canonized in 1622 by Pope Gregory XV.

*Happy Fault*

During the Exultet, the great hymn of the Easter Vigil, the cantor sings of the "happy fault" of the sin of Adam which "gained for us so great a Redeemer." Ignatius's wounded leg was also a "happy fault." As the young knight was carried on a litter to his family home, in severe pain with a shattered leg, he must have felt great despair and fear. Would he ever engage in his chivalric deeds again? Were his dreams of glory forever shattered? Would he even walk again?

Due precisely to this leg injury, however, Ignatius had the time and the grace to reflect on who he had been and who he wanted to become. Reading and meditating upon the lives of Christ and the saints deeply affected him and opened his soul to God. The vision of the Blessed Virgin deepened his desire to grow closer to God and to give his life in service. Rather than hindering his life, the leg injury and long convalescence transformed his life. So too we can let our illnesses and disabilities become our "happy faults."

*Ignatius as Companion*

Whether dealing with a short- or long-term illness or disability, Ignatius of Loyola is a fine companion. Ignatius would certainly understand the fears of anyone being rolled into the operating room, having experienced repeated painful procedures himself. Anyone remaining in bed for long periods of time could turn to Ignatius of Loyola, knowing that he experienced the same. Reading his *Autobiography* and recognizing the tremendous good that flowed from his temporary disability will help one with any illness or injury become aware of the seeds of grace in his or her own situation.

God continually bestows grace on us; we, however, *choose* whether or not to open ourselves to it. Ignatius responded to the grace by turning his convalescence into an extended prayer time. After some initial resistance, he kept his gaze on God by embracing fully the "tools" of grace God offered: spiritual reading and active use of the imagination. All of us today, well or ill, can follow his example by getting into the habit of regular spiritual reading. A spiritual life that includes spiritual reading is a decided asset in growing closer to God.

*Graced Imagination*

In his masterpiece of Western mysticism, *The Spiritual Exercises,* Ignatius of Loyola gives us an additional effective tool for growing closer to God: "the graced imagination." Using our imagination, just like the young Ignatius, we can enter into a Gospel scene by praying with it. We can choose the perspective of a person in the scene or place ourselves there as we observe Jesus closely. We watch as he continually reaches out to the marginalized people of his day, we listen carefully to his words, and we feel the suffering of his Passion. By paying close attention to Jesus through prayer of the imagination, we will grow ever more like him.

Illness in its varied forms and the many levels of disability are universal parts of life. As so often happens, though, God's grace can transform the darkest human experience into brilliant shining light. For Ignatius of Loyola, God worked through his lengthy convalescence slowly but emphatically, eventually transforming a worldly young knight into a devoutly spiritual future saint.

As Ignatius's story clearly shows, God invariably uses our difficult life experiences to better us in some way, to help us grow. Many people who have had a bout with serious illness have noticed that it has made them more compassionate toward others' physical conditions, more aware of their own dependence on God, more prayerful and alert to suffering in general.

The temporary disability and long convalescence of Ignatius of Loyola demonstrate quite clearly that illness can transform not only our lives, but also our souls. The human spirit is magnificently resilient and, through the grace of God, can transform the physical challenges of illness and disability into unimagined spiritual treasures.

## five

BLESSED KATERI TEKAKWITHA
*Our Companion in Physical Disfigurement*
(1656–1680)

*I*magine how beautiful it was back then. Mile after mile of unbroken wilderness containing pristine lakes and streams, clear untainted air and trees of every kind and description. This was North America before the Europeans came to colonize, cultivate and convert.

For many centuries this North American wilderness was inhabited only by wild animals and indigenous peoples who had migrated there from Siberia. Over the following centuries these early Americans evolved into quite distinct groups: Iroquois and Algonquin in Northeastern America; Aztec and Mayan in Central America. Both the Algonquin and Iroquois peoples eventually broke down further into tribes: the Iroquois included Mohawks, Senecas and Oneidas; the Lenape, Cree and Montagnais tribes were Algonquin. These tribes of Native Americans lived in the eastern half of the United States and Canada, each having its own customs, religious practices and sometimes languages. The Iroquois tribes lived with several families together in structures they called *longhouses*. One thing all tribes shared, however, was the wise use of the land, water and majestic forests that their Great Spirit had given them. They realized that their livelihood depended upon their stewardship of these precious resources.

And just as the pine, birch and maple trees of these majestic forests dropped their seedlings upon the dark earth, so God dropped a most unexpected "seed-gift" into this seventeenth-century, North American landscape. The tiny infant girl named "Tegahkouita" or "Tekakwitha" ("one who advances or cuts the way before her")[1] was born in 1656 in the Iroquois village of Ossernenon, the same village where the North American martyrs Saints Isaac Jogues and René Goupil had died four years earlier. Against many odds, this tiny girl would become an outstanding model of gospel values, known as "The Lily of the Mohawks," inspiring all whose lives she touched and continues to touch to this day.

From the time she was born, Kateri Tekakwitha (as she would be known after her baptism) was different because of her dual heritage: Her mother was from an Algonquin tribe, while her father was an Iroquois Mohawk. The Algonquin and Iroquois tribes did not coexist peacefully; in fact, they were bitter enemies. Members of these different Native American tribes did not intermarry. Kahenta, mother of Kateri Tekakwitha, however, had been taken captive during an Iroquois raid on her Algonquin village, located near modern Quebec. Mohawks tended to use their captives brutally, marching them back to their own village where they were either tortured and put to death or, if they passed muster according to the village matriarchs, permitted them to live as slaves.

Kahenta, however, was fortunate. She was not only spared torture and death, but because of her beauty and gentle manner, the chief of the village fell in love with her and chose her as his wife. While little Kateri Tekakwitha was born an Iroquois princess, her mother Kahenta had quite a different lifestyle: She had been baptized by the Jesuit "Blackrobes" in her former village and was a Catholic.

Kateri's parents soon had another child, a son. Native American mothers were generally kind and loving to their children, and Kateri's mother was no exception. What *was* highly unusual, as well as dangerous, however, was Kahenta's passing on to her young daughter instruction in Christianity, most likely at great personal risk.

*Iroquois Religious Beliefs*
In order to understand the Mohawks' resistance to Catholicism, it is important to understand Iroquois religious beliefs. The Mohawks already had their own quite sophisticated religion. They believed in a supreme being whom they called the "Great Spirit." Every village had a group of elders, aptly named "Keepers of the Faith," who presided over village morality as well as religious ceremonies. The Iroquois people strongly believed in caring for those who were weak among them—elders, orphans and any who were ill. Also, they held regular religious rituals that were based on the cycles of nature. One such festival, called "The Maple Dance," was always preceded by a "Meeting for Repentance," during which the people apologized to one another for any hurts they had caused and vowed to reform. The Mohawk people believed in an afterlife and performed elaborate burial rituals, including the beautiful symbolism of setting loose a bird during a burial ceremony to represent the soul's journey to heaven.

Although the Mohawks were kind and loving to one another, they also had a dark side. They were extremely fierce warriors and performed brutal tortures on captives for days, often cutting out the heart of a victim, sometimes while the person was still alive, and eating it. For all their elaborate religious rituals, they had no concept of the Christian ideal of loving one's enemies. In light of their own highly developed religious beliefs, it is easy to see why the Mohawk chiefs resented what they viewed as an imposition of another religion on their people.

The chiefs also had an additional reason for resisting the Jesuit missionaries. In the seventeenth century North America began to be visited more and more by English and Dutch fur traders hoping to become rich. France also sent its fur traders, and along with them, Jesuit missionaries. While some native tribes had an amicable relationship with the Europeans, the Mohawks did not, resenting the white man's increasing encroachment upon their game and lands. While certainly the French Jesuits had missionary rather than monetary motives, to the Mohawks they were as dangerous as the fur traders.

*Kateri's Illness*

Kateri Tekakwitha's illness occurred while she was still a young child. When she was four years old, disaster struck Tekakwitha's village in the form of smallpox, the deadly infectious disease that the European colonizers had carried over with them. Called "the purples" for the terrible rash it caused, smallpox ravaged the Iroquois, who had no resistance to it. Even strong warriors among the Mohawks in Ossernenon succumbed, sometimes keeling over and dying right in the village square.

Sadly, tiny Tekakwitha's parents and little brother died from the ravages of smallpox, leaving her an orphan. Tekakwitha herself contracted the disease and lingered close to death for months. Although she survived, the disease literally marked her for life. "Kateri recovered slowly, but she was heavily pock-marked, and her eyes no longer had their merry lights or their loveliness. She was half blind, reduced to seeing all creatures in shadows."[2]

Soon after Kateri's recovery, her tribe moved from Ossernenon to a new settlement at Caughnawaga, near Auries Creek, New York. This move was probably necessary for general health reasons for all who had survived the terrible smallpox epidemic. At Caughnawaga, Kateri participated in the same daily activities as all Iroquois children did. Her aunts taught her how to do the fine Mohawk embroidery with colorful beads and quills that were beloved by her tribe. Despite her impaired vision, Kateri Tekakwitha became famous for her skill in decorating moccasins and clothing with her own unique designs.

For the rest of her short life, Kateri Tekakwitha lived with the dual disabilities of impaired vision and severe facial scarring. These disabilities naturally affected Kateri, lowering her self-esteem and causing her to become shy and reserved; she preferred indoor duties around the hearth to the outdoor chores that brought her into social contact with her peers. Indeed, the fact that she always drew her shawl up closely around her face to hide her features tells us that she was self-conscious, aware that her facial scars made her different from other young Mohawk women.

The scars on her face very likely became scars on her soul, deep wounds that marked her interaction with others. However, as we have seen throughout this book, God uses these wounds we all bear—illnesses and disabilities or other "soul scars" of being human—as sources of grace and transformation. As Saint Paul says, "for whenever I am weak, then I am strong" (2 Corinthians 12:10). So often the "weaknesses" that we struggle with are precisely instruments that God uses to strengthen us and draw us close. It would have been easy for Kateri to withdraw completely from village life and become bitter. Instead, she eventually accepted her disabilities, allowing God to work through them and transform her into a woman of genuine holiness.

*Refusal to Marry*
As we have seen, the Iroquois possessed a strong moral ethic of caring for their weaker members. After the death of Tekakwitha's parents when she was only four years old, her uncle and aunt immediately adopted her into their family as one of their own children.

Like their European counterparts, Mohawk women were expected to marry. Marriage ensured that the tribe would continue and that there would be enough people to do the work of hunting and caring for the crops. Well before her baptism, Kateri resisted marrying. As we do not have any autobiographical account from Kateri herself, we do not know the precise reason for her not wishing to marry.

Did her facial disfigurement cause this reluctance? Did she have an inner sense that remaining celibate could dispose her to God more? Whatever her motive, Kateri handled the difficult situation wisely. She never refused outright to marry; she simply avoided the topic when it was brought up.

Finally, her aunts and the matriarchs of the village decided that the time had come to address the situation. They arranged for a young warrior of the village to visit Kateri. Her aunts asked Kateri to serve the warrior a bowl of porridge, a symbolic gesture that would indicate Kateri's acceptance of the man in marriage. However, Kateri immediately rose and left her longhouse, thereby rejecting this attempt to marry her off.

*Conversion to Kateri*

Kateri's adamant refusal to marry did not endear her to the women of her village. They began to torment her, always giving her the most demeaning and difficult domestic tasks. Kateri accepted this treatment humbly, doing what she was asked without complaint.

Now it was time for the life-giving water of God to flow onto the seed of holiness God had planted among the Mohawks. Although the Jesuits had been banned from Caughnawaga for several years, they had left bits and pieces of the faith behind. Kateri surely heard the tales of the Blackrobes who had been martyred in the same village where she was born. Perhaps fragments of the stories they told about Jesus were quietly repeated from time to time. Most likely something remained in Kateri's heart from the lessons of her Catholic mother. Due to her "soul scars" of weak vision and facial scarring, Kateri's tendency to withdraw into solitude gave her ample opportunity to absorb and reflect on what she had heard.

Things changed when the chiefs of Caughnawaga reluctantly permitted the Jesuits to return in 1670. Father Jacques de Lamberville, s.j., ministered zealously among Kateri's people, using scenes from Christ's life painted on bark to overcome the language barrier. Slowly, some of the Mohawks began to convert to

Catholicism. Contrary to what we would expect for a future saint, Kateri did not initially come forth, pleading to be baptized as her mother had been. Instead, true to her retiring nature, Kateri stayed quietly in the background for a few months, listening to Father de Lamberville talk about Jesus. Kateri's relationship with God was a spousal one, and at this point she was a young maiden entranced, shyly observing and drinking in all she could about the One with whom she was in love. Her desire for baptism grew.

One day Father de Lamberville passed Kateri's longhouse while she was inside recovering from a slight wound. On impulse, and undoubtedly inspired by the Holy Spirit, the priest entered and began to converse with her. To his surprise, this quiet young Mohawk girl opened her heart to him, speaking of her parents, her already considerable knowledge of Christianity, her choice of celibacy and, finally, her wish to be baptized. The missionary Jesuits normally were reticent about baptizing their new converts, preferring to wait many months to see if the person had a genuine call to Catholicism. However, after providing a relatively short period of instruction and querying other villagers as to her character, Father de Lamberville accepted Kateri into the faith. To her joy, the young Mohawk maiden was baptized on Easter Sunday, 1676, being christened "Catherine" after Saint Catherine of Siena, or "Kateri," as we know her today.

### Grace and Firewater

We have already seen the devastating effects that the smallpox disease brought by the Europeans had on the Iroquois people. An even more lethal disease brought and fueled by the Europeans was alcoholism. Again, the Native Americans had no experience of, and thus no resistance to, alcohol. Occasionally, the people of Caughnawaga would embark on drunken sprees, to the point of injuring themselves and others. Despite being cautioned about the dangers of "firewater" by the Jesuits, the villagers, including women and children, began to drink more frequently.

Kateri, who quickly began developing a deep prayer life, found these drunken sprees appalling. She had always been able to commune with God, but after receiving the sacrament of baptism, grace flooded her soul and she became even more prayerful and desirous of time with her Lord. After falling in love, it is natural to desire companions with whom to share that love. Kateri tried her best to live her faith in the midst of the debauchery around her, praying the rosary she always carried and refraining from working on the Sabbath.

These practices of Kateri began to turn the villagers, including her own family, against her. She was roundly mocked, earning the derisive name "The Christian." Once she was threatened by a young warrior with a tomahawk, who ordered her to cease her Christian ways or he would kill her. Kateri remained calm, thereby defusing the situation. After she told Father de Lamberville what happened, he became increasingly worried about her, finally advising her to leave Caughnawaga for a safer Jesuit mission. This was much easier said than done, however. Kateri's uncle, the chief of the tribe, would not hear of her leaving, beginning again to pressure her to marry a Mohawk warrior.

*Kateri's Journey*
Kateri eventually found a way to make a dramatic escape from Caughnawaga. Once, while her uncle was away, three other Christian Native Americans visited her village. With the assistance of Father de Lamberville, Kateri was spirited away in their canoe. Returning soon afterward, her uncle, enraged, embarked in his own canoe in close pursuit. While Kateri was hidden in the woods, one of her companions signaled to her uncle to come ashore. The uncle did so, and discovered only an elderly man smoking his pipe. Admitting defeat, Kateri's uncle returned to Caughnawaga. She never saw him again.

By this journey, Kateri Tekakwitha was honoring her mother's life and faith, not only by returning to the North from where her mother came, but by fleeing to a place where she could openly practice her

Christianity. Kateri's flight from Caughnawaga has biblical overtones, echoing the escape from death of the child Moses who was placed in a basket of reeds and also floated down a river to a new life. Father de Lamberville gave Kateri a letter for the Jesuits at her new mission that read, "I send you a treasure, guard it well."[3]

*Deepening Relationship*

Kateri's new home was called St. Francis Xavier of Sault St. Louis, located not far from Montreal. Generally known as "The Sault," the mission contained a chapel and homes for the priests inside a strong stockade. About 150 Native American Christians lived just outside the walls. The Sault mission had a reputation as a model of Catholic community in the New World. Life there revolved around the worship of God: Two Masses were celebrated each morning, one at dawn and one at 8:00 AM. At 3:00 PM all gathered to pray the Liturgy of the Hours of Vespers, followed by Benediction. Catholics from as far away as France came to witness this deep piety and profound love of Christ, so unexpected in the American wilderness.

At the Sault mission, the Christian converts were expected to live like Christians: to take the words of Jesus to heart, to live as he had showed us how to live. This meant more than merely going to Mass and saying prayers; it meant that one had to live the Christian virtues: kindness, prayerfulness, humility and concern for others. The two Jesuit priests, Father Cholonec and Father Chauchetière, were accustomed to the Mohawks at the Sault who lived a good Christian life. So at first they saw nothing unusual in their new arrival, except that she drew her shawl more closely around her face than other Mohawk women did.

After being mocked and tormented at Caughnawaga for so many months because of her Catholicism, Kateri Tekakwitha must have been ecstatic about her new life. At the Sault mission, she was able to worship and share her love of God freely with other Mohawk converts.

*Kateri's Spirituality*

The tiny God-seed that had managed to survive among the drunken brawls and cruel treatment in Caughnawaga now began to blossom into the "Lily of the Mohawks." One of the more highly regarded Mohawks at the Sault Mission was Anastasia, who had known Kahenta, Kateri's mother. Anastasia, a devout Christian matriarch, gladly took Kateri, the daughter of her old friend, under her wing, suggesting that Kateri remove the colorful and gaudy beads that all unmarried Iroquois women wore in their hair. Kateri at once complied, removing the ornaments and telling Anastasia that she was doing it for the Blessed Mother. This action demonstrated not only Kateri's acceptance of whatever would bring her closer to God, but also indicated the deep inward change she was experiencing because of her conversion.

Living in this holy atmosphere of structured worship, surrounded by genuinely devout people, was like having the holy water of God flowing over and nurturing the seed of Kateri's contemplative nature. Kateri attended the first Mass at dawn and remained in the chapel for the second Mass. She fell to her knees every time the Angelus, the great prayer of the Blessed Mother, rang. "Unrestrained by the forces which had made her life so difficult in her village, Kateri used the chapel services and the natural loveliness of the surroundings to practice all of the Christian ideals which had formed in her heart in secret for so many years."[4]

*Prayer Life*

While we have no firsthand account of her prayer life from Kateri herself, we are fortunate to have the next best thing: an account from her spiritual director and confessor, Father Cholonec. Father Cholonec, also the head of the mission, began to realize that his colleague Father de Lamberville's statement that Kateri was a "treasure" was indeed correct. Kateri was different from the other Sault converts in that she attended both daily masses at the Sault, exhibited unusual zeal in her daily devotions and was regarded by all as genuinely holy.

As her spiritual director, Father Cholonec gradually recognized that Kateri's focus was genuinely on God rather than on herself. Her hours of prayer in the chapel were sincerely God-centered, with the fruit of this prayer apparent in the way she lived: quietly fulfilling any duty, no matter how humble; speaking of God as often as she could; and always demonstrating deep kindness to others. In light of all this, Father Cholonec decided to permit her to receive Holy Communion, an unusual step in an era when Communion was distributed infrequently.

*Kateri as Mystic*

As Kateri's spiritual director, Father Cholonec knew also that Kateri was a mystic, able to pray in a profoundly contemplative way.

In the book of the prophet Hosea, God says, "Therefore, I will now allure her, / and bring her into the wilderness, / and speak tenderly to her" (Hosea 2:14). Sometimes God leads us away from all we hold dear so that we may hear God more clearly in a "wilderness" experience. This is often the "lemonade" we can make while experiencing a "lemon" in time of sickness or temporary disability. After we stop resisting and wondering "Why me?" and start to settle down our spirits, God can speak quietly in the depths of our hearts.

With Kateri Tekakwitha it was different. Not only did she live in an actual wilderness, with the mighty forests as her cathedral and the quiet coves as her chapel, but she also lived in a wilderness of the heart resulting from her self-image. Even before receiving the sacraments, Kateri's disabilities had helped her develop a contemplative spirit, able to focus on God in the beauty of creation and the beauty of her own heart. She had developed an ability to listen, to observe, to see God in nature, and God used this ability of Kateri's to lay the foundation for her contemplative spirit. After the grace of her baptism, and fostered by the Christian atmosphere of the Sault, Kateri became a genuine mystic. This was apparent in the way she lived her prayer life, seeking solitude and contemplation, as well as living the Christian virtues of compassion, humility and love.

Just as moths naturally flutter toward candlelight, so do people move instinctively toward another who clearly emanates Divine Fire. For a time, Kateri suffered from being falsely accused by another woman at the Sault of a flirtation with that woman's husband. She bore this slander gracefully, knowing correctly that she would eventually be exonerated. After this incident, the other Iroquois converts began to recognize that they were in the presence of a genuinely holy woman, one in whom the flame of Divine Love burned brightly. They naturally began drawing closer to her in order to glimpse the God she so loved. For the second time in her short life, Kateri Tekakwitha was known as "The Christian." This time, however, the appellation was uttered not derogatorily, but with the utmost respect.

*Spiritual Friendship*

We are not called to live out our spiritual journey alone. Jesus told his disciples, "For where two or three are gathered in my name, I am there among them" (Matthew 18:20). God often blesses us with friends of the heart, persons with whom we can easily and naturally share our souls. Kateri was fortunate to have not only the village matriarch Anastasia as her mentor, but also a woman closer to her age named Marie Theresa. Marie Theresa had lived a difficult life, having lost her husband to starvation during a blizzard and struggled with her own Christianity. Kateri and Marie Theresa first met soon after Kateri arrived at the Sault. Together they decided to devote their lives to Christ: Marie Theresa out of a spirit of repentance, Kateri because she simply could do nothing else.

On one occasion, Kateri and Marie Theresa visited the Montreal mission, which was larger and more established than the Sault. Montreal had a hospital, founded by the Hospital Sisters, and schools for both native and French children. Deeply impressed by the God-centered lifestyle of these sisters, Kateri and Marie Theresa returned to the Sault with the intention of starting their own religious community. When they proposed the idea to Father Cholonec, he was highly amused by the thought of Iroquois nuns and virtually laughed in their faces. He was unconsciously expressing the racism of the time: The Native Americans were there to be evangelized, not to become evangelists themselves. Even his awareness of Kateri's profound spiritual gifts made no difference. A few years after Kateri's death, however, Marie Theresa did start a religious community of Iroquois women modeled on the life of her friend, Kateri.

Kateri and Marie Theresa accepted Father Cholonec's decision calmly and continued their daily prayer practices and sharings together. Kateri, however, did set her heart on one aspect of religious life: She wanted to publicly formalize her deep love for Jesus by professing a vow of perpetual chastity. Although astonished, Father Cholonec consented, and on the feast of the Annunciation, March 25, 1679, Kateri Tekakwitha consecrated her virginity and purity of soul to Christ. While we do not know for certain, she perhaps also vowed to sanctify her disabilities by joining them with the wounds of Jesus, thus furthering her deep union with him.

*Last Days*
One day, while Kateri was out in the forest gathering firewood, a large branch fell from a tree and struck her on the head, knocking her unconscious. Kateri regained consciousness and returned to the mission, but the accident seemed to give her a premonition that her time on earth was growing shorter. She did not fear death, neither did she wish it to come sooner: God's will was her will.

In early 1680 Kateri, never robust since her childhood bout with smallpox, began to visibly weaken. It became clear to all at the Sault that their "Christian" was dying. Members of the mission sat by her pallet, caring for her and seeking her spiritual counsel and guidance. Father Chauchetière began to visit Kateri often, as Father Cholonec was busy with mission affairs. They had lengthy conversations about spiritual matters. Father Chauchetière, realizing that Kateri was literally on heaven's doorstep, invited the children of the mission to come and listen to Kateri speak about her love for Jesus.

One day Kateri, to Father Chauchetière's amazement, asked him to draw a picture of her. He protested, claiming he was not an artist. Kateri persisted, and Father eventually produced the only known rendition of Kateri. This request demonstrates Kateri's spiritual and emotional growth. Her intimacy with Jesus soothed the scars on her soul, helping her accept, and even love, her physical appearance enough for her to want to show the world who she was. Her disabilities, formerly sources of low self-esteem, had become sources of grace and union with Jesus. Her weakness had become her strength.

By Holy Week of 1680 Kateri was in severe physical pain and clearly dying. On Tuesday she received the Eucharist in the form of Extreme Unction. The next day, April 17, 1680, at only twenty-four years old, Kateri Tekakwitha, with the names Jesus and Mary on her lips, died peacefully in her longhouse.

Then something amazing happened.

To the utter astonishment of all present, Kateri's facial scars disappeared. Before the Iroquois residents of the Sault now lay a young woman transformed, with strikingly beautiful features and translucent skin, showing the Lily of the Mohawks in her final, full bloom. This transformation illustrates the words of Saint Paul: "Even though our outer nature is wasting away, our inner nature is being renewed day by day" (2 Corinthians 4:16). It was as though God said, "See, you saw her scars. But this is the beautiful soul that I saw all along."

Shortly before her death, Kateri had said good-bye to her spiritual friend Marie Theresa: "I shall love you in heaven. I shall pray for you. I shall aid you."[5] Kateri knew her destiny was heaven, and that she would continue her ministry of spiritual guidance of others from there.

*Kateri as Companion*

Almost all of us are unhappy about one or another aspect of our appearance: a too-long nose, too-thin hair, too short, too tall, too fat. Or there may be other reasons for the scars on our soul, for why we feel different from others. When we feel this way, we have a choice— we can withdraw into our pain and remain there, or we can follow the example of Blessed Kateri Tekakwitha and allow our woundedness to strengthen us. For Kateri, wounded in so many different ways— orphaned, scarred, partially blind, rejected for her faith—allowed her soul scars to strengthen her and bring her close to Jesus. Her places of struggle were themselves the graces, the instruments of fertilization that God used to bring the Lily of the Mohawks to full bloom.

And, as she told her friend Marie Theresa, she will aid us from heaven, she will pray for us, and she will love us.

Let us take her up on it.

## six

SAINT THÉRÈSE OF LISIEUX
*Our Companion in Terminal Illness*
(1873–1897)

$S$he entered the cloister at fifteen, became novice director at nineteen, died after an agonizing bout with tuberculosis at age twenty-four and was canonized in the record time of twenty-eight years. Most recently, she was proclaimed a doctor of the church by Pope John Paul II in 1997, only the third woman to be so honored. Although she received little formal education, her spiritual writings are still read all over the world.

She is Thérèse of Lisieux, one of the most beloved saints of the Catholic church.

The young Carmelite, also known as "The Little Flower," has earned her tremendous popularity because her "The Little Way of Spiritual Childhood" has taught countless people that it is not necessary to engage in complicated spiritual practices to grow close to God. Thérèse's "Little Way" instead emphasizes great love, humility and trust in God—attitudes of heart available to all. Her autobiography,

*Story of a Soul,* illustrates that Thérèse herself lived this way: lovingly, humbly and rooted in radical trust in Jesus.

The same radical trust was sorely tried when Thérèse had a lengthy and painful bout with illness: her year-and-a-half-long struggle with the tuberculosis which finally took her life in 1897. Thérèse's radical trust also invites all who contend with illness and disability to reflect deeply on this profound grace and to look to her life for counsel and companionship.

Regarding pain, weakness and debilitation, there is no doubt that Thérèse of Lisieux "walked the walk." In the midst of intense physical agony, this extraordinary young Carmelite exhibited not only profound trust in God but also remarkable joy in suffering. At the same time, she did not deny or negate the physical pain caused by the slow disintegration of her lungs from the tuberculosis—an agony not unlike the experience of crucifixion, which also suffocates the lungs. Thérèse is certainly a saint to lean on for anyone who lives with wrenching physical pain, overwhelming fatigue or physical limitation of any sort.

*Background*

The facts of Thérèse's life are well-known. Born January 2, 1873, into an extremely devout family in Normandy, France, she was the youngest of five daughters. Both parents, before meeting, had considered religious life but did not enter for various reasons. Interestingly, each one of their children joined a cloistered community—four to the Carmel at Lisieux and the fifth, Leonie, to the Visitandines in Paris. Thérèse, the youngest, was a bright and precocious child, much loved by her family.

Thérèse knew illness almost from the day of her birth. As an infant, she was so sick that it was deemed necessary to place her in the countryside with a wet nurse for continual care. Shortly after her much-loved older sister Pauline entered the Carmelite convent at Lisieux, twelve-year-old Thérèse became ill with an apparently psychosomatic "nervous disease" that involved severe headaches and seizures. However, it is the manner with which she dealt with her final illness—the tuberculosis that wasted her lungs and slowly suffocated her to death—that has much to teach anyone today who contends with significant physical suffering.

At a mere fifteen years of age, responding to God's call, and perhaps relying on some deep inner instinct that her life would be brief, Thérèse Martin petitioned the Prioress at the Lisieux Carmel, her pastor, her bishop and even Pope Leo XIII for permission to enter the Carmel. Despite the dual obstacles of her young age and already having two sisters in the Lisieux Carmel (the church was reluctant to have too many members of one family enter the same cloister), Thérèse was finally granted the necessary permission. She joined her sisters Pauline and Marie on April 9, 1888.

Neither the fact that her father had suffered a stroke nor the poor food and famous cold of the Carmel had any obvious effect on Thérèse's health in her early years there. However, Thérèse had been prone to colds and sore throats while growing up, and the damp Normandy climate, combined with the hardships of the Carmelite lifestyle—lack of sleep, continual cold and poor food—eventually began to take their toll on Thérèse. At several points during the latter half of 1894, Thérèse's sore throats and husky voice were so bad that they required treatment: Her sister Celine, who had entered the Lisieux Carmel in 1895, cauterized Thérèse's throat several times with silver nitrate.

While the experience of having one's throat coated and cauterized with silver nitrate is decidedly not a pleasant one, it foreshadowed what was to come: Thérèse's bout with the tuberculosis that took her life.

*Tuberculosis*
It is interesting to speculate how Thérèse contracted tuberculosis. Tuberculosis is an airborne disease that was quite common in the

nineteenth century, generally transmitted by coughing and speaking. As the Martin family was notoriously insular (none of them seems to have had it) and not one of the other Carmelites ever contracted tuberculosis, it is likely that Thérèse contracted it from someone with whom she lived. Generally, tuberculosis *is* contracted this way. However, as one biographer points out, none of the other Carmelites ever became tubercular: "No one, not even the doctor, seems to have thought of the danger of contagion; Thérèse continued to take part in the community life, ate at the same table with the other nuns, used the same dishes and tableware, helped with the laundry."[1] Since tuberculosis can remain dormant for years, perhaps she was exposed to it on a pilgrimage to Rome that she had made earlier.

We may reasonably conclude, though, that the lack of nourishing diet, continual cold and insufficient sleep—the hallmarks of the Carmelite cloister—weakened Thérèse and made it more difficult for her body to fight the disease. Sadly, after having been on the decline, tuberculosis made a resurgence in the 1980s and remains a major public health concern to this day.

While we may never know exactly how Thérèse got the disease, we do know precisely when its first definite symptom appeared. On the eve of Good Friday, April 3, 1896, Thérèse coughed up blood for the first time. The next morning, she dutifully reported this incident to the Prioress, Mother Marie de Gonzague, who sent for a doctor. The doctor, however, was only able to perform the most cursory of examinations through the cloister grille and thus failed to recognize the seriousness of the situation. Thérèse continued her duties as a Carmelite for another year, even as her fatal disease went untreated.

Although Thérèse appeared well (and never complained to the contrary), the tuberculosis continued its destructive work under her placid exterior. During Lent of 1897, her body began to succumb to the tuberculosis, which became quite pronounced. The cloister's doctor applied the standard treatments: mustard plasters, iodine paintings and cauterizations. Thérèse was relieved of her charges and given a better diet. Now that the severity of her condition was apparent, her natural sisters were given permission to tend to her needs.

## Thérèse's Dying

We are fortunate that the dying of Thérèse of Lisieux is as well-documented as the rest of her life. Her three natural sisters in the Carmel not only took care of her but, aware of her spiritual greatness, wrote down everything she said in the final stages of her illness.

The modern reader, especially the modern reader with an illness, tends to read with some skepticism the account in *Story of a Soul* of Thérèse's response to her first hemoptysis, or coughing up of blood: "I didn't know what it was, but I thought that perhaps I was going to die and my soul was flooded with joy."[2] Looking forward to death with joy is certainly an alien attitude: Is this some bizarre over-romanticizing of death? Is it a suicidal tendency no one suspected? Is she in denial of what would lie ahead? Or is her spiritual dimension so highly developed that she did not have normal, human responses to illness and death?

The answer to each of these questions is a decided "no." We must look at Thérèse's reaction in the context of who she was, a young Carmelite with an extremely mature spirituality. The following words provide a clue to Thérèse's thinking: "I was interiorly persuaded that Jesus...wanted to have me hear His first call. *It was like a sweet and distant murmur which announced the Bridegroom's arrival.*"[3] As the imagery clearly shows, Thérèse was anticipating her eternal wedding far more than her earthly funeral. From her earliest years, her love for Jesus was profound. *Story of a Soul* is filled with her repeated declarations of her love for God. Her response, then, to the first concrete sign of the illness that would end her earthly life but unite her soul with her beloved Jesus forever, as unnatural as it seems to us, was quite natural for Thérèse of Lisieux.

Through the summer of 1897, as the tuberculosis relentlessly progressed, Thérèse experienced fever resulting in dehydration, continual difficulty breathing, extreme weakness (making her unable even to make the sign of the cross), bedsores and intestinal gangrene. While today's treatment for tuberculosis is painless, the remedies of the nineteenth century were literally as painful as the condition itself: vesicatories (hot plasters placed on the skin to cause blistering) and "pointes de feu" (red-hot needles used to puncture the skin). In addition, Mother Marie de Gonzague would not permit morphine to be given to Thérèse: "She had inflexible, old-fashioned views on the grave moral effects of this anodyne and believed it was not proper to stupefy a Carmelite nun with such things."[4] (Interestingly, Mother Marie de Gonzague's "old-fashioned views" may not be so old-fashioned. Today's medical establishment is still cautious about prescribing morphine to people with intense physical pain, for fear of addiction.) As a result, the last five months of Thérèse's life were sheer agony.

*Radical Trust*

Again, Thérèse is a premier teacher of the radical trust in God that is so necessary when dealing with serious illness. In May of 1897, as the final stages of the disease were beginning, Thérèse said to Mother Agnes (her sister Pauline): "I haven't any misgivings whatsoever about the final struggles or sufferings of this sickness, no matter how great they may be. God has always come to my aid; He has helped me and led me by the hand from my childhood. I count upon Him. I am sure He will continue to help me until the end."[5]

Thérèse was well aware how ill she was. Since tuberculosis was as common in the nineteenth century as cancer is in the twenty-first, she recognized that death from tuberculosis was a harrowing one. Instead of reacting in fear by dwelling on the horror ahead, she chose instead to focus her trust on God: "God gives me courage in proportion to my sufferings. I feel at this moment I couldn't suffer any more, but I'm not afraid, since if they increase, He will increase my courage at the same time."[6] This remarkable statement by Thérèse was made on August 15, 1897, six weeks before her death. She was candid about what she was going through (at this stage the tuberculosis began to spread to the left lung, causing severe pain and making breathing even more difficult), stating that she could not conceive of any more suffering, but also realizing it was God giving her the strength she required.

In spite of her already prodigious sufferings, Thérèse had the utmost faith that, should her suffering increase (and increase it did), God would provide her with the necessary graces. Again, the level of faith that Thérèse is exhibiting at this point should inspire all with illness to ask God for the same sustaining grace.

*Joy in Suffering*
Along with trust, Thérèse had the wonderful capacity to find joy in suffering. Joy is different from happiness. Happiness is a transitory emotion; joy is a spiritual stance toward life, a contentment and peace that come only from God. Her sister Marie, in a letter to her uncle Monsieur Guerin, described Thérèse's capacity for joy in the midst of her dying process: "Then she began amusing herself by talking about everything that would happen at her death. Because of the way she did this, whereas we should have been crying, she had us bursting out with peals of laughter, so amusing was she.... I believe she'll die laughing because she is so happy."[7]

In *Story of a Soul*, Thérèse herself testifies to her joy-filled suffering: "I have suffered very much since I was on earth, but, if in my childhood I suffered with sadness, it is no longer in this way that I suffer. It is with joy and peace."[8] It is difficult for us to understand how this is possible. How can someone be so joyful while experiencing such physical agony? Thérèse shows us the formula: Suffering when joined with intense love for God provides a joy that no earthly pain can disturb. Put simply, when we love someone deeply enough, we will suffer for that person. And Thérèse demonstrates this again and again in her embracing of suffering with Christ throughout her life. She says, for example, of her entrance into Carmel: "Yes, suffering opened wide its arms to me, and I threw myself into them with love."[9]

One of Thérèse's poems again shows her love of God as well as her abandonment to God:

> Love, that fire of our Fatherland,
> Never ceases to consume me.
> What matters life or death to me?
> My sole happiness is to love You only.[10]

Life *or* death—neither mattered to Thérèse. Her poem is not merely pious romanticism. The young Carmelite's profound love for God was obviously the bedrock of her life. The poem closely resembles Ignatius of Loyola's famous prayer of the Principle and Foundation: "we should not prefer health to sickness...a long life to a short life"[11] but be open to *whatever* leads to a deepening relationship with God. This is the deep spirituality and intense love for God that so many great mystics had.

Thérèse of Lisieux did not deny the reality of her human condition—she experienced the discouragement that accompanies pain and illness. About six weeks before her death she acknowledged her despair, but also her hope: "How easy it is to become discouraged when we are very sick! Oh, how I sense that I'd become discouraged if I didn't have any faith! Or at least if I didn't love God."[12] How many times have we all prayed like this? Yes, it *is* easy to become discouraged when dealing with illness or serious disability, yet at the same time it is comforting to realize that Saint Thérèse of Lisieux felt the same way. What a wonderful spiritual companion this young saint can be, inviting us again and again to transform despair through hope.

"My little life is to suffer, and that's it!... God knows best what to do with these sufferings; I've given them all to Him to do with as He pleases."[13] With these words, Thérèse invites us to make our suffering worthwhile, as she did, by giving it to God. By doing so, we emulate not only her, but the Jesus she loved so dearly, the Jesus who suffered and died for us all. Her suffering was prodigious. Due to difficulty in breathing and swallowing, there were times when Thérèse was unable to receive Communion. This was a great spiritual deprivation, as she loved receiving the Eucharist. However, this also gave Thérèse the opportunity to learn a great spiritual lesson: "Without a doubt, it's a great grace to receive the sacraments; but when God doesn't allow it, it's good just the same; everything is a grace."[14]

Thérèse is a genuine companion and superb role model for those of us who live with different but just as debilitating illnesses in contemporary manifestations, such as cancer, AIDS or autoimmune conditions. Thérèse knew that illness is as infused with the potential for divine grace as any other human experience. "All is grace"—this phrase, which has become a spiritual slogan for Thérèse of Lisieux, reminds us all that even the excruciatingly hard things can lead us to God.

*Remarks of Others*
No one lives in a vacuum. Each of us is connected to others—family members, spouses, friends, coworkers, neighbors. The bonds that are generated by the daily rubbing of elbows in religious life are also strong. Religious are naturally aware of the opinions and concerns of the women with whom they live. As Thérèse's life and death are so well-documented, we also have much information about the interaction among the Carmelites of Lisieux. Thérèse, possessed of a sensitive heart, also felt keenly the experience of dealing with the remarks and comments of others. As anyone with a physical condition knows well, people feel utterly free to make judgments, offer opinions as to how ill one really is or ought to be and give advice.

The young Carmelite learned early the importance of ignoring such unsolicited remarks of others. A few days after Thérèse received the habit, one sister felt moved to remark how plump the young novice was; shortly after, another sister commented about how thin Thérèse was getting. Thérèse's response to these two opposing appraisals was quite wise: "Ever since that moment, I have never attached any importance to the opinion of creatures."[15]

This profound, though difficult, spiritual advice is for all of us, particularly those of us who are unwell. When dealing with the unwanted comments of how we are so pale, thin, fat, short, weak, strong or anything else, it is well to remember Thérèse's advice: The opinions of "creatures" simply do not matter. It is who we are in the eyes of God that is important—the God who loves us, not *despite* being pale, thin, fat, short, weak, strong or whatever, but *because* of it.

It was fortunate that Thérèse was indifferent to others' opinions of her, for she greatly needed this grace during the time of her illness. One can almost hear the exasperation in her voice when she exclaims: "Last week, I was up and around and some found me very sick; this week, I'm no longer able to stay up; I'm exhausted; and they judge me to be on the mend! What does it all mean!"[16] Anyone with a chronic condition knows exactly how she feels.

*United With Christ in Suffering*
Another incident shortly before Thérèse's death illustrates how the young saint handled unwanted behavior from others. Every evening during Sacred Silence, a sister would sit at the foot of Thérèse's bed and laugh at her. (Our most charitable interpretation of this is that perhaps she was trying to cheer up the dying Thérèse.) When her sister Pauline remarked about this unusual behavior, Thérèse replied, "Yes, it's painful to be looked at and laughed at when one is suffering. But I think how Our Lord on the Cross was looked at in the same way in the midst of his sufferings.... This thought aids me in offering Him this sacrifice in the right spirit."[17] She acknowledges her emotional

pain, but then she immediately turns to Christ on the cross and turns her struggle over to him. Thus, she offers us a powerful spiritual lesson: Suffering, whether physical, emotional or spiritual, can be made holy when we unite our pain with that of Jesus. When experiencing a loss of our own dignity, we can remember Thérèse turning her humiliation into an opportunity to become united even more closely with Jesus. We can turn to her in our hearts and ask her to pray with us for the same grace.

*Strain on Others*

Another concern that is universal for all of us with serious illness or disability is our physical care, and the financial and emotional strain that providing care will put on the lives of family and friends. Thérèse was no exception. She was concerned about the financial cost of her illness for her religious community. Relying primarily on donations for its existence, the Carmel at Lisieux was very poor, like most Carmelite convents to this day. Caring for someone through a long, protracted illness requiring costly remedies was a severe drain on scanty resources. And, of course, there were no Medicare or national health programs at that time.

In addition, Thérèse was not able to put in the eighteen-hour workday and prayer that everyone else did. Naturally, she was very aware of her inability to contribute to the operation of the Carmel. Again, those of us with chronic conditions which keep us from working full-time can identify: It can be a decided blow to our self-esteem not to be able to contribute as much as our colleagues do. When feelings like these surface, we can recall Thérèse's "Little Way," which stressed loving God with all one's heart and performing the humble tasks of life with love and humility. We can love God wholeheartedly in any life situation, from a hospital bed or wheelchair, when adjusting to hearing aids, or while experiencing the loss of vision that can accompany aging.

*The Death of Thérèse*

Finally, on September 30, 1897, her agony was over. After a year and a half of enduring the slow suffocation of tuberculosis, Thérèse of Lisieux struggled for her last breath. The account of her death is extremely moving. At 7:20 in the evening, surrounded by her three natural sisters and the other sisters of the Lisieux Carmel community, she clutched her crucifix tightly and exclaimed while looking at it: "Oh! I love Him!... My God...I love you!"[18] She then placed her head down and died.

It took several minutes to remove the crucifix from her hands.

*Roses*

Pictures of Thérèse usually show her holding a bouquet of roses. Tradition holds that Thérèse answers requests for intercession by sending a rose to the petitioner. This tradition is rooted firmly in Thérèse's story. She had a great love of flowers: she uses the metaphor of flowers for her family in the beginning of *Story of a Soul* and often refers to herself as a "little flower" throughout the text. When her sister Pauline was expressing sorrow at Thérèse's impending death, Thérèse responded, "Oh no, you will see; it will be like a shower of roses."[19]

She has been true to her word. There are myriad stories worldwide about favors being granted through the intercession of Saint Thérèse of Lisieux, usually accompanied by a manifestation of a rose. The rose does not necessarily come delivered to one's front door by a florist or an angel, but may be on a greeting card, a bush by the road or "appear" in other subtle ways. Again, while not official church doctrine, the rose and Thérèse are irrevocably linked in the popular imagination.

*Thérèse as Companion*

Thérèse was sure that her ministry would continue in heaven. Shortly before she died, Thérèse assured Pauline that she would spend her time in heaven doing good upon earth. Part of this includes being a spiritual companion to those of us who turn to her. Thérèse knew well how excruciating pain can drain body and soul; she did not try to minimize her profound suffering while in conversations with her sisters. When in pain, who better to ask to intercede for us before God for the grace we need than this young Carmelite who experienced such an agonizing death? She will reach out to take the hand of anyone seeking her companionship; she will surely understand our struggles with despair and invite us to imitate her example of radical trust.

Yes, because she was a cloistered religious whose life centered on Jesus, turning to the Lord came more naturally to her than to others. Yet this is precisely why the church gives us saints—to show us different paths to God. We don't have to live in a cloister to be close to God; we need to pray and ask for whatever grace we need most. Turn to Thérèse and ask her help. When discouraged, ask for the grace of hope. When overwhelmed by pain, try to imitate Thérèse's giving her pain to God.

"Tout est grace"—all is grace. Whether in French or in English, this advice from Thérèse of Lisieux is spiritually priceless. With these words, Thérèse invites us to turn the tables on the biggest challenges we face: illness, grief, addiction, divorce. No matter the form of suffering, Therese beckons us to call on her and let her show us her little way of daily, radical trust in God.

And who knows? Someday, in a place you would least expect, you may just stumble across a rose.

## seven

VENERABLE MATT TALBOT
*Our Companion in Alcoholism*
(1856–1925)

irst his life centered on drink, then his life centered on God. Venerable Matt Talbot was a simple Irish laborer from the day he was born in 1856 to his death in 1925. He would certainly have lived the same ordinary life as his contemporaries were it not for the disease of alcoholism. Matt Talbot was not someone who did things by halves. For as fervently as he devoted himself to drinking in his young years, he just as fervently gave the rest of his life to God.

*Early Life*
Matthew Talbot was born on May 2, 1856, in the North Strand section of Dublin, home to thousands of poor, working-class people, many of whom had migrated there during the famine of the 1840s. His father, Charles Talbot, a hardworking man of short stature and large temper, was fortunate to have steady employment on the Dublin docks. Elizabeth Talbot, his mother, who had been a domestic servant in the village of Clontarf, just north of Dublin, eventually bore ten more children, nine of whom lived to maturity.

Going to school was an on-and-off proposition for low-income Dublin children at that time. Matt and his brothers attended the O'Connell school, administered by the Christian Brothers. His attendance was sporadic, resulting in about a fourth-grade education.

At age twelve, Matt took his first job and his first drink. He worked as a messenger for E. and J. Burke, a wine and beer establishment in Dublin. With so much alcohol available, it was not uncommon for the workers to "take a drop" for themselves now and again. So Matt began his lengthy journey with the demon of alcohol at a very young age. It was not long before the twelve-year-old boy was coming home drunk. His father tried to dissuade him from drinking with a severe beating, but it did no good. Matt was well on his way to becoming a raging alcoholic; the path had already been set.

Charles Talbot, himself a heavy drinker, had worked on the Dublin docks for many years. Now, aware that his son was in trouble, he got Matt a job in the same firm where he worked, in order to keep an eye on him. This also failed to curb Matt's heavy drinking, which soon became an embarrassment to his father. Matt tried to quit drinking to spare his father this continual embarrassment, but his heavy drinking continued.

Matt's next job was as an assistant to bricklayers, which involved carrying heavy loads of bricks up and down ladders and over rough ground. As Matt's friend Pat Doyle said, "He was a good hodman; everyone had to give him the palm for that.... When he was with...the builders, he'd do more in half-an-hour than the rest would in an hour."[1] The foremen usually put him in the forefront of the work in order that he set the pace for the other men. By now in his late teens and a full-blown alcoholic, he unfortunately set the pace in the pub, too.

### The Demon

Alcoholism in Ireland was a major problem in Matt Talbot's day. Dublin contained at least two thousand pubs. In 1865 police arrested 16,192 Dubliners for drunkenness, a third of them women; nineteen people actually died from alcohol poisoning in 1866.[2] No wonder alcohol was called a demon.

The Catholic church in Ireland was well aware of the havoc alcohol wreaked on the lives of its people. Several priests of the time were renowned for preaching against "intemperance" and encouraging people to "take the pledge" against drinking. A major factor that kept many Dubliners from taking this pledge was the fact that laborers were paid in the pubs, with the underlying assumption that most of the money would then be spent in the pubs. Invariably, most of the money was.

Alcohol was certainly a major problem in Matt Talbot's life. He spent almost every cent he made on drinking, giving the barman at his favorite pub his entire wages so that he could drink until his money ran out. As this usually happened by the middle of the week, Matt did what he had to do in order to keep drinking, including sponging off his friends in the pub. Meanwhile, there was rarely any money left over for the running of the large Talbot household. At times desperate for a drink, Matt often came home without his boots or his shirt, having sold them. He and his friends would play a trick on a woman barkeep, several of them standing together in front of a barrel while one reached in to steal some of the pig's cheeks inside. Then they would sell the pig's cheeks and go drinking. The worst thing that Matt ever did, and something he regretted for the rest of his life, was stealing the fiddle belonging to a man who was blind and earned his meager income playing music in the streets. As Matt was decidedly not a mean-spirited man, this action shows how terrible his craving was for alcohol. "From his early teens until his late twenties, the pattern of Matt Talbot's life was that of the drunkard, lost to self-respect, deaf to the appeals of a heart-broken mother, a slave to the craving for alcohol, a workman who in his hours of leisure drank not only his hard-won earnings, but any other money that he or his drinking companions could raise."[3]

*Alcoholism the Disease*

Despite the many stigmas still attached to it, alcoholism is an illness. If left untreated, severe cases may eventually result in death. Alcoholism is a complex disease, involving hereditary aspects, emotional factors and, most importantly, the makeup of the brain. Alcoholism's symptoms include loss of control over how much one drinks; physical dependence; insatiable craving; and building a tolerance to the alcohol so that one has to drink more and more to feel its effect.

While people have been abusing alcohol for millennia, alcoholism and other forms of addiction were not considered diseases until 1784, when Dr. Benjamin Rush of Philadelphia published a pamphlet that examined the effects of chronic drunkenness. He argued that the condition was an illness, rather than a moral failing, stating that it is a primary disease that affects one's mental, emotional, physical and spiritual life. The American Medical Association declared alcoholism an illness in 1958.

One of the saddest effects of alcoholism is its ability to change one's personality. When an alcoholic is open to the grace to stop drinking, it can be like peeling off the mask that concealed the real person inside. Matt's niece, Susan Fylan, states: "He was a changed man immediately after taking the pledge. We never heard him swear again.... His workmates were astonished when they heard of Matt taking the pledge; and they were still more astonished when he kept it."[4]

As craving a drink is one of alcoholism's hallmarks, it is no wonder that Matt's friends were astonished that he never drank again. To counteract his craving for alcohol, Matt got into the habit of walking after work. One evening he passed one of his old hangouts, and only his tremendous strength of will, along with the grace of God, kept him from entering. He instead turned and went into a nearby church.

Sometimes God sows the seeds of our conversion in subtle ways. Although Matt Talbot was an alcoholic, he was also a man of integrity.

The fiddle incident gnawed at his conscience. Not long after stealing the fiddle, Matt's life changed. One Saturday night the twenty-eight-year-old Matt and his brothers, also heavy drinkers, were out of money. They went to the pub anyway, expecting their drinking pals to treat them to a pint or two. Perhaps their friends were low on cash themselves, because the expected offers never came. Matt was highly offended and trudged home, telling his mother he was going to take the pledge to stop drinking. His mother, no doubt surprised to see her son home early and sober, told him, "Go, then, in God's name, but don't take it unless you are going to keep it." Matt responded, "I'll go, in God's name." As he left, his mother said, "God give you strength to keep it."[5]

God answered Elizabeth Talbot's prayer. "Keep it" he did. Matt Talbot never took another sip of alcohol the rest of his life.

*Treatment for Alcoholism*
Precisely because alcoholism is so complex and affects so many aspects of a person's life, treatment for it must also be broad. The first phase of treatment is entirely medical, as the withdrawal process with its accompanying symptoms of depression, nausea and even hallucinations can be extremely difficult, even dangerous. Alcoholics today usually detoxify in a safe medical setting such as a hospital. Medical supervision was not available to Matt, but he was gifted with a strong will that allowed him to endure his withdrawal symptoms stoically. The fact that Matt confessed to his mother several times that he would drink again after his three months were over testifies to his struggle with withdrawal.

While there is no cure for alcoholism, the detoxification phase of treatment is just the beginning; it is followed by either a stay in a rehabilitation facility or an intense outpatient program. The intense outpatient program includes meeting with an addictions counselor several hours a day, as well as attending Alcoholics Anonymous, a worldwide fellowship of support meetings based on the Twelve Step

Program. Rehabilitation also includes getting a sponsor, an individual more experienced in dealing with the baffling aspects of sobriety and working through the twelve steps.

Alcoholics Anonymous (AA) was founded in America within a decade of Matt Talbot's death by Bill Wilson, a man who had a similarly severe drinking problem. Bill Wilson was on the verge of alcohol-induced dementia in 1935 when he met an alcoholic physician named Dr. Bob. The Twelve Steps, the cornerstone of AA, were written by Bill Wilson and the early members of AA. Bill Wilson sought to compose an accurate set of principles that would stress confession, self-survey, prayer, an ongoing relationship with God, helping and making amends to others and carrying the AA message to other alcoholics.

*Discovering God in Addiction*

Of course there was none of this in 1884. Matt Talbot had to deal with the symptoms of withdrawal and trying to stay sober alone, with no AA group, no sponsor, no addictions counselor available to him. He did, however, have one very decided asset in combating his alcoholism: a deepening relationship with God.

Until this point, Matt Talbot had been an indifferent Catholic, still attending Mass, but not receiving any sacraments for several years. As an alcoholic, Matt's god was the bottle, and his altar was a bar. And Matt had worshiped well. Even during his years of heavy drinking, God's hand was on him. Years later he told a friend that even when drunk he would remember Mary and say a prayer to her. God's goodness was in his heart, and God's love as expressed in the patience of his mother was the backdrop of his life.

As we have so often seen throughout this book, God will use the challenge of illness to draw us close. That was certainly the case with Matt Talbot. Matt's efforts to stay sober drew him into an intimate relationship with God. The day he stopped drinking was the day of his genuine conversion. His Catholicism changed from the mere faith handed onto him by his parents to a mature relationship with Jesus

Christ and his mother Mary. His daily life focused more on his relationship with God and his unknowingly drawing others to God by his continual example of holiness. The energy and tenacity he formerly devoted to slaking his thirst for alcohol was now poured into slaking his thirst for God.

Viewed from the outside, Matt's life did not change much. He continued "setting the pace" as a manual laborer, fetching and carrying building materials for the more skilled craftsmen. On the inside, however, Matt was a changed man: "From the little that is known of Matt Talbot between the years 1884 and 1891, there emerges a man intent on humbling and hiding himself, a soul mindful of its every step...diligent and constant in his occupations, spiritual and temporal."[6]

Matt was nothing if not diligent in his spiritual practices. The first Monday after taking the pledge, Matt shocked his family by rising early for 5:00 AM Mass before going to work. Daily Mass became his routine. The hours that he had formerly spent in pubs he now spent in church. He would kneel on the steps outside the church for thirty minutes or more before it opened for liturgy, and he often spent entire days there on weekends. He was faithful to the usual Catholic devotional practices: the Stations of the Cross, a fifteen-decade rosary and the Angelus three times daily. He joined many sodalities and other Catholic groups, and donated much of his earnings to charity. Matt also quietly pursued penitential practices and austerities such as eating very little food and sleeping on a plank instead of a mattress. The fact that Matt Talbot was indeed a changed man eventually became apparent to all.

*Matt's Steps*

Although Matt's sobriety began almost fifty years prior to the founding of Alcoholics Anonymous, in many ways he was already practicing many of its ideals. AA advises members to change "people, places and things" in order to keep sober. Matt's sister, Mary Andrews said, "He usually spent Saturday afternoons away from where he might meet his old companions, and generally in a church."[7] Matt also embarked on an ambitious program of spiritual reading, which must have been quite the challenge for him since he was barely literate.

Matt was also practicing several of the Twelve Steps before they were ever written. Step One asks the recovering alcoholic to admit being powerless over alcohol. Step Two acknowledges that only "a Power greater than ourselves can restore us to sanity."[8] Matt Talbot's continual emphasis on God after taking the pledge clearly shows that he realized his powerlessness over his drinking and that God alone was stronger than his craving to drink.

Step Five asks recovering alcoholics to "[admit] to God, to ourselves and to another human being the exact nature of our wrongs."[9] Although Bill Wilson was not a Catholic, he was describing in effect the sacrament of reconciliation, confessing one's sins to God through a priest. After his conversion, Matt Talbot frequently went to a Jesuit priest, Father James Walsh, for confession. Step Nine recommends making amends with anyone we have caused harm through use of alcohol. Matt made a point of repaying all his old pub debts, quietly placing the money on the bar and leaving quickly. He spent many years looking in poorhouses for the man from whom he stole the fiddle, but never located him. Instead he had Masses said for him.

Matt Talbot practiced Step Twelve thoroughly: "Having had a spiritual awakening as a result of these Steps, we tried to carry this message to others, and to practice these principles in all our affairs."[10] As we have seen, Matt's spiritual awakening was a profound one. He focused his life entirely on God. Although Matt made a strenuous effort to get his brothers and some of his drinking companions to reform as he did, he was not successful. After some time, realizing that living with other men who drank was not helping his sobriety, Matt moved out to his own rooms. Anyone using a Twelve Step program invariably realizes that personal integrity and self-scrutiny, the underlying principles of the Twelve Steps, begin to affect not just his recovery program but all areas of his life. Matt Talbot became known by his family and friends as a man of integrity in all matters. One of his nieces said of him: "All he cared about was the principle that a promise should be kept and that a debt should be paid."[11]

As Bill Wilson discovered, alcoholics respond much better to the experience and strength of another alcoholic than to a nonalcoholic. Thus the concept of sponsorship is important in the Twelve Step program. Clearly, there was no AA sponsor for Matt Talbot, but the Holy Spirit led him to a wise priest, Monsignor Michael Hickey. Monsignor Hickey served as Matt's spiritual director and friend; they spent long evenings together discussing spiritual matters, singing hymns and talking about God. Father James Walsh remained his confessor. Matt intuitively realized the value of spiritual companionship in staying sober.

*Al-Anon*

We have already seen that in his drinking days Matt was in the habit of giving his paycheck to the pub, resulting in there being no money to help his parents. On one occasion, Matt handed his mother a shilling, saying "Here, mother, is that any good to you?" His mother replied, "God forgive you, Matt. Is that the way to treat your mother?"[12] Life for Elizabeth Talbot must have been a continual struggle. Her husband drank, as did all but one of her sons: "The men of the family all had more or less regular employment; but, though they could have lived in comparative comfort, the fact that all were steady drinkers— Matt and Phil heavy drinkers who contributed little or nothing to the household budget—must have kept the family income in a sadly depleted state."[13] The Talbot family moved eleven times in twenty-five years, an indication that, despite the older children's employment, there was too often not enough income to pay the rent. Elizabeth Talbot, mother of ten, worked as a charwoman to make ends meet.

*Is that the way to treat your spouse, mother, father, child, sister, brother, friend...?* Elizabeth Talbot's cry of anguish echoes in many families today. Those who care about an alcoholic often ride the same merry-go-round of anger, guilt, accusation, emptying liquor bottles, worrying, doubting their own sanity at times as Elizabeth Talbot no doubt experienced. Perhaps more than any other chronic illness, alcoholism affects the entire family.

Many years after Bill Wilson and Dr. Bob founded AA, Bill's wife, Lois, realized the deep need that family members of alcoholics also had for recovery from alcoholism. In her memoir, *Lois Remembers*, she wrote: "The big lesson I have learned is that we cannot change another human being—only ourselves. By living our own lives to the best of our ability, by loving deeply and not trying to mold another to our wishes, we can help not only ourselves but that other also."[14] Realizing the critical need for family and friends of alcoholics to come together for mutual support, Lois Wilson founded Al-Anon in 1951.

People typically come to Al-Anon looking for specific "cures" and ways to manage the alcoholic, but gradually learn that the only people they can change in life are themselves. After working the Twelve Steps and learning that he did not cause the disease, cannot control the disease and, certainly, cannot cure the disease, Al-Anon members can begin to regain hope and find serenity even when living with an active alcoholic.

### Matt's Death

Matt spent several months in the hospital with a heart and kidney condition in 1923. At first, his doctor wondered if Matt was some type of religious crank, but after recognizing Matt's deep spirituality and focus on God, the doctor eventually became convinced that his patient was a truly holy man. After being informed by his doctor that he could die a sudden death at any moment from heart disease, Matt, now sixty-five years old, was discharged from the hospital.

And that's the way it happened: God called Matt Talbot home on

Trinity Sunday, June 7, 1925. Dublin was in the midst of a heat wave. A neighbor noticed Matt did not look well and almost followed him, but changed his mind, for Matt was not the type to like any kind of fuss. Walking to St. Saviour's Church, Matt turned into Granby Lane, stumbled and fell to the ground. People rushed to his aid but realized he was dead and sent for a priest, who administered last rites. Matt's body was taken to the hospital, where, since he carried nothing except a rosary and a prayer book, he was not immediately identified. Soon, however, his sister missed him and went to the police. Matt's funeral was small, attended only by his family and a few friends.

*A Societal Problem*

Matt Talbot would have remained a virtually anonymous Irish laborer like thousands of others of his day if it were not for one unusual ascetic practice. When his body was undressed in the hospital, it was discovered that he was wearing chains. This discovery startled hospital personnel and the fact that a simple laborer had practiced the ancient asceticism of quietly wearing chains on his body soon spread throughout Dublin

As we live in an era of instant self-gratification and continual comfort, it is difficult for us today to understand why someone would engage in such an extreme practice. Matt, however, chose to live in the ancient tradition of Irish monasticism, known for austere mortifications of the body. The goal was to discipline the body in order to make the spirit more receptive to God's invitation to prayer. Today many spiritual directors invite people instead to deepen their prayer lives by uniting the sufferings they already experience with the sufferings of Jesus on the cross. And it is precisely here that Venerable Matt Talbot has much to offer as a spiritual companion.

Alcoholism causes as much suffering today as it did in nineteenth-century Ireland. According to the National Council on Alcoholism and Drug Dependence, about eighteen million Americans have alcohol problems. More than half of all adults have a family history of alcoholism or family drinking; almost half of all traffic accidents are alcohol-related.[15] In addition, alcoholism has other severe societal consequences: domestic violence, employment problems, homelessness. Its impact on family life is devastating, especially for children: "Those of us who grew up in families affected by alcoholism were particularly vulnerable to its effects because the disease touched us early in our lives.... We learned not to talk, not to trust, and not to feel."[16] Fortunately, alcoholism is treatable today, but only with the full cooperation of the alcoholic and family members affected by the alcoholic's drinking.

While knowledge this explicit was not known in Matt Talbot's time, Matt himself knew that his alcoholism was taking over his life. We have seen how Matt responded to the abundance of grace bestowed on him by the Holy Spirit, allowing it to guide him on a God-centered path. As his spiritual life deepened, he set out on his program of asceticism in a spirit of repentance: the intensity with which he drank was channeled into a program of prayer and asceticism that made him an intimate of Christ.

*Matt as Companion*
Had Matt Talbot had the opportunity to remove his chains before he died, the holiness of his life would never have been known. Shortly after his death, interest in this unusually holy old man spread quickly throughout Dublin and the rest of the world. Biographies were written, as people wanted to know more about his life. Interest in Matt Talbot as a holy person continued to grow until finally in 1931 a Tribunal was established to formally investigate his life for future sainthood. He was declared venerable in 1949 by the Catholic church.

Whether or nor Matt Talbot is ever declared a canonized saint by the Catholic church, he is definitely a saint to many recovering alcoholics. One recovering alcoholic, Philip Maynard, has written a book called *To Slake A Thirst, The Matt Talbot Way to Sobriety,* which emphasizes the importance of a deep relationship with Jesus for recovering alcoholics. There are also Matt Talbot Retreats, which focus on Matt's life and spiritual recovery along with the Twelve Steps.

And what a spiritual companion he is to anyone dealing with alcoholism! Matt Talbot lived with its darkness—the cravings, dependence, the alcohol taking complete control of his life—and understood how baffling a problem alcohol can be. He knew the importance of placing God firmly in the center of his life and invites all of us to do the same. Recovering alcoholics can be assured that Matt Talbot keeps a watchful eye on them, interceding on their behalf before God. He is delighted when they turn to him learning about his life and seeking his friendship. He is even more delighted when they imitate his example by turning to Christ in the sacraments, deepening their personal prayer lives and making a sincere effort to apply the spiritual wisdom of the Twelve Steps to *all* aspects of their lives.

And for the multitude of people who live with or care about an alcoholic, Matt Talbot also knows the mayhem alcohol causes in your life. He invites you to take care of your own emotional needs and to remember that the only person you can change in life is yourself.

Matt Talbot was not the founder of a new religious community, nor did he travel to foreign lands to convert people to Catholicism; rather, he was an ordinary Dublin laborer dealing with a difficult disease. Through extraordinarily heroic effort, he was able to detach himself from his cravings for alcohol and attach himself deeply to Jesus Christ and Mary, his mother. Known by his fellow workers as one who set the pace for others to follow, he set a pace in his spiritual life that not only conquered his alcoholism, but turned him into a most worthy spiritual companion.

Let Matt Talbot help set the pace in your life.

## eight

CARYLL HOUSELANDER
*Our Companion in Mental Illness*
(1901–1954)

JULY 21, 2004

ear Alexis,

How nice to hear from you. You're right; it has been a long time since we connected. Yes, it *is* true that I'm writing a book about holy people and how they are spiritual companions to those of us with illnesses and disabilities. The communion of saints has always fascinated me—it's an ancient belief from the early church. The early Christians were convinced that their beloved dead were still in close connection with them.

I'm thrilled that you're in a group for people with bipolar disorder. I think a group of understanding people can be a great support. As you know, living with depression or any type of mental illness is not easy. Other people just do not understand how incapacitating depression can be. Considering how common mental illness is, it is good that we have much better treatments now with new medications as well as psychotherapy.

You asked if there is someone in the communion of saints who would be a good spiritual companion for you. I think I can suggest the ideal person—Caryll Houselander, an English author of the twentieth century. She was born in England to Gertrude Provis and Willmott Houselander in 1901.

Her best-known book is *The Reed of God,* a beautiful book about the Blessed Mother. Caryll Houselander was quite gifted. She wrote many poems and books and was also an artist, specializing in woodcutting. In my view, she is not only a spiritual writer of great insight, but also a genuine mystic for our times. Indeed, she had a profoundly deep spiritual life but was also quite human and had endearing flaws like smoking, swearing and making unkind remarks about others (which she greatly regretted later). It is things like this that make her so easy to identify with.

Most of all, though, Caryll Houselander possessed keen insight into the nature of the human psyche and very much identified with persons with mental illness, as she felt she herself suffered "neurosis" (the word used in the 1920s and '30s for many different emotional conditions). Indeed, her letters to her numerous correspondents, edited by her biographer and friend Maisie Ward, are filled with her descriptions of her own various emotional conditions. Here are a few samples:

· "I do know all about the terrible depression you speak of, as I suffer from it too, and have done so ever since I was nine years old or so...."[1]
· "If you have this anxiety complex (I myself have it too, by the by)...."[2]
· "I am a frightened, abject creature, because in youth I was broken right across (psychologically!) early and irrevocably...."[3]
· "I also was for years a chain smoker—used actually to stay up most of the night so as to go on smoking...."[4]
· "I also took to starving myself as a very young child, and later as an adolescent...."[5]

Caryll certainly experienced a variety of emotional struggles. She was definitely a "wounded healer": knowing quite a bit about different emotional states of mind because she had been there herself. While it is difficult to gauge the severity of her conditions, what *is* clear is that she not only viewed herself as a "neurotic," she was clearly drawn to others with mental illness. Many troubled individuals sought her out for advice; she often visited a home for mentally ill persons in London, and she was adept at healing young boys who had been traumatized during World War II. Eminent London psychiatrists sent patients to her for informal "social" therapy, which, according to one of them, meant she "loved them back to life." *Love* is so important for all of us— to both give it and receive it. And although popular music constantly sings about romantic love and its feelings, love is really more about *giving* than about feeling good.

Many blessings,

*Janice*

P.S. The official patron for mental illness is Saint Dymphna from the sixth century. See if you can check out her story.

. . . . .

SEPTEMBER 13, 2004

Dear Alexis,

Greetings from Philadelphia! As always, good to hear from you again. I agree with your assessment about Saint Dymphna. Her story is certainly tragic, and it does cast the person with mental illness in an unfavorable light. After all, Dymphna herself is a victim of her father's sickness—he had her murdered for refusing to marry him. Certainly a sorry tale about the effects of mental illness.

I'm glad you are beginning to get to know Caryll by reading about her life in *That Divine Eccentric*. What I love about her is that she saw more than the illness; she saw the whole person, and in particular the Christ in the person. In her autobiography *A Rocking-Horse Catholic*, she recounts the extraordinary mystical experience which permeates her writings and is the touchstone of her spirituality. As a young adult, Caryll was ambivalent about the Catholic church after being humiliated by a church usher because she didn't have the penny required for the pew rental. Despite this, she still "longed for the Blessed Sacrament and the beauty of the liturgy of the Church."[6] Just as she was beginning to give in to the temptation to leave the church for good, God granted her an extraordinary vision:

> I was in an underground train, a crowded train in which all sorts of people jostled together, sitting and strap-hanging— workers of every description going home at the end of the day. Quite suddenly I saw with my mind, but as vividly as a wonderful picture, Christ in them all. But I saw more than that; not only was Christ in every one of them, living in them, dying in them, rejoicing in them, sorrowing in them—but because He was in them, and because they were here, the whole world was here too.[7]

This intense religious experience lasted for several days: "I came out into the street and walked for a long time in the crowds. It was the same here, on every side, in every passerby, everywhere—Christ."[8] As so often happens with religious experience of this depth, God gradually unfolded its life-changing meaning to Caryll:

> It would be impossible to set down here all the implications of this "vision" of Christ in man; it altered the course of my life completely.... To trust Himself to men, that he may be their gift to one another, that they may comfort him in each other, give Him to each other. In this sense the ordinary life itself becomes sacramental, and every action of anyone at all has eternal meaning.[9]

Her experience of seeing Christ in all persons *was* truly life-altering—Caryll Houselander not only returned to the church herself, she converted many others throughout her life. Also, she became much less judgmental about others, especially self-righteous Catholics, than she had previously been, realizing: "It did not dawn on me that in condemning others wholesale as Pharisees, I myself was a Pharisee."[10]

It is so easy to smugly judge others, when if we knew what they were dealing with, we'd be so much more understanding. I know that people with mental illness are the brunt of much misunderstanding because their actions (like sleeping a lot when deeply depressed) are seemingly abnormal. It's hurtful when others, especially family members, refuse to believe a person is mentally ill, but sometimes I wonder if they're in denial? Or afraid? If a relative has serious depression, what could that mean for them and for their children?

What deeply touched Caryll Houselander in her mystical experience was the realization that Christ was truly in *everyone,* every human person on earth. This epiphany greatly intensified her already-present tendency to be drawn to those people who lived on the fringes of life: "I knew too that since Christ is One in all men, as He is One in countless Hosts, everyone is included in Him; there can be no outcasts."[11] Thus, being inclusive of *everyone* became a primary theme not only of her writing, but also of her life.

I urge you to continue to get to know Caryll Houselander—read her writings if you can get them, but also try to talk with her in your prayer. She will understand!

Love,
*Janice*

. . . . .

OCTOBER 11, 2004

Dear Alexis,

I'm glad you find Caryll Houselander helpful, as I believe she is definitely the modern patron of mental illness. She's so honest about her flaws: a "workaholic," perfectionist, anxious and depressed at times, but ministering to others out of these very weaknesses. She's certainly a model for taking the pain of life and using it to build the kingdom of God. Plus she enjoyed a glass of gin from time to time!

The realization that Christ is in everyone led Caryll to a profound love for the church's doctrine of the Mystical Body of Christ. This is an ancient doctrine of the church that teaches that we not only are united with Jesus through the church, but are also *united with one another*. The implications are clear—we are to love God, but also our friend, neighbor, enemy—for not only is Christ present in everyone, but each of us is mystically linked to one another as the Body of Christ. In one of her letters Caryll writes: "In the Mystical Body we are all one, and we do all experience the Passion in a thousand secret ways, and we share—if we want to or not—in each other's lives and responsibilities."[12] What a beautiful way to view not only those around us, but also all of humanity—especially during these days of terrorism masquerading as acts of God!

In her love for the Mystical Body, Caryll gives us much fruit for meditation. *Every* person, no matter what the physical or mental difficulties, is united to Jesus. I'm going to put on my spiritual director hat for a moment and invite you to feel what it is like for you to be united to Jesus. Are you aware of how close he is at every single moment, especially the dark ones? Can you feel deep in your soul how he longs to have you turn to him?

And for me, it has been an eye-opener to realize that not only is Jesus in everyone, even the people I find difficult, but that *I* am joined to *them* in Christ. We are all connected: to him and to each other. Personally, I find it very challenging to try to *understand* the people in my life and not automatically reject the ones I find difficult. It reminds me how much Christ loves them, and how I am called, hard as it is at times, to see *everyone*, even the people who don't like me, in terms of their wounds, not their faults.

Also, I believe that this realization that Jesus lives in each and every one of us is quite important for people with mental illness. No matter how you are treated by others, you will *always* retain your innate dignity because Jesus the Christ resides in you. Hopefully all people will also realize that every person, despite their emotional disabilities and the sad stigmatization that accompanies mental illness, reflects Jesus and thus should be treated with respect and dignity.

Blessings,
*Janice*

. . . . .

NOVEMBER 25, 2004

Dear Alexis,

Thanks for your note. I know it can be a struggle to write when depressed. Did you know that scholars speculate that Emily Dickinson's "I felt a funeral in my brain" is a description of depression?

Caryll Houselander was keenly aware of the stigma and the marginalization that people with mental illness too often live with. In a letter written in June 1948, she writes movingly how her visit to a home for mentally ill people touched her deeply, and also spoke to her of the inclusive Mystical Body:

> I've seldom, if ever, been present at anything so moving as the prayers in the tiny Catholic chapel in the evening, organized entirely by the patients, the prayers of their own choosing and

said aloud: and what a mystery and what an example—an ex-
Trappist monk, a young girl, an old lady bent double nearly, but
in spite of it and of being insane, beautiful, and a handful of
others—all people who had started out in life intent on a high
vocation, and given it indeed—utter abnegation, put away in a
lunatic asylum. And this is the point—they reached out in their
prayers to the whole world. As I knelt among them, listening at
first and in the end joining in unconsciously with them, I grew
more and more amazed at their petitions:
"For Russia"
"For the suffering people of Europe"
"For the sick"
"For prisoners"
"For the conversion of the world"
"For purity of heart in the world"
"For purity of heart here"—
and then, to me the most moving petition of all, "That we
here in this little chapel dedicated to Your divine Heart may
have perfect abandonment to Your dear will."[13]

As most of us are not in the habit of seeking out mentally ill people,
this experience says a lot about Caryll Houselander's deep desire to
be in the presence of persons living the mystery of mental illness. As
she was so keenly aware of the Christ in everyone, Caryll was able to
see the residents of the home as full human beings, individuals with
specific histories and gifts—a "beautiful old lady" or "ex-Trappist
monk." To her they were *people*, not patients. Caryll could recognize
not only their spiritual gifts (despite their severe mental conditions,
they were obviously rooted in God and had a deep desire for prayer)
but she also saw the spiritual foundation, the "utter abnegation" of
their lives. And Caryll Houselander had the grace to be humbled by
her time with the residents: the global scope of their other-centered
petitions impressed her.

Caryll's letter continues with a lyrical summary of the whole experience:

> "…it was simply an almost unbelievable showing of the heart of the Mystical Body of Christ, literally bleeding before God with the wounds of the world!"[14]

Clearly, she was gifted with the spiritual insight to describe the experience in terms of what it was—some of the most marginalized members of the Mystical Body interceding before God with the needs of the world. Caryll's a wonderful heavenly companion not only for persons with mental illness, but also for anyone with a friend or family member with the condition.

Today, of course, institutions have been scrapped in favor of group homes for individuals with mental illness. To me, this makes much more sense—who wants to live in an institution? It's so easy to become just a room number in a large impersonal facility. This is why the disability movement is lobbying to get the long-term care system revamped so that people who don't want to go into a nursing home will be able to stay in their own homes. Plus, the government would save money because home care is definitely cheaper.

Blessings,
*Janice*

. . . . .

DECEMBER 15, 2004

Dear Alexis,

I do so enjoy hearing from you. Your bipolar support group sounds great. I've found that when living with a disability the support of others who truly understand is crucial. Actually, Caryll Houselander said it quite well: "One doesn't want a preacher or even a shining example, but someone who will share the burden."[15]

Alex, I'm glad you are enjoying *That Divine Eccentric,* Caryll's biography. For living a relatively short life, Caryll Houselander certainly had an interesting one. I was impressed with her courage during the London Blitz—being a fire-watcher most of the night and then working in First Aid posts infested with the mice she was so terrified of! She also wrote so much—her bibliography numbers over seven hundred items, mostly articles she wrote for Catholic periodicals. She certainly was prolific!

As I said before, I feel she will be remembered not only for her writing, but also for her articulation of a spirituality of mental illness. Caryll was certainly familiar with suffering, having had both physical and emotional conditions in her own life. Since she was there herself, she could empathize with others: "Never has any spiritual adviser more sincerely said, more profoundly felt, a oneness with those she was advising."[16]

In my humble opinion, what is most important in Caryll Houselander's spirituality of mental illness, however, is that she could see the spiritual value inherent in mental conditions. As Maisie Ward points out in *That Divine Eccentric,* Caryll Houselander recognized *that the suffering that accompanies mental illness is just as redemptive as the suffering that accompanies any other type of disability or illness:* "All Christians realize this about the [disabled], the physically sick, the old and feeble—but Caryll saw the redeeming Christ also in lunatic asylums and in mental homes."[17] The theme of mental illness as not only Christian suffering, but also as *redemptive* suffering definitely runs through Caryll Houselander's work: "For neurosis is a tremendous, redemptive suffering. Its place in the Christ-life is Gethsemane."[18]

This has tremendous spiritual implications for all people with mental illness. This unique suffering is as sacred to God as any person's physical suffering. Everything that is difficult—the struggle to be functional, dealing with the shame associated with mental illness, the lack of understanding from mentally healthy persons—can be gathered up and offered to the Lord for the healing of the world. This suffering is not in vain—it has profound healing value. Or, as Caryll herself says: "Remember...that it is at the sore place, and only there, that our healing begins; and that whenever healing does begin at a sore which you have had the courage and love to expose, there, in that sore spot, the healing of the whole world begins."[19]

The church, indeed, most Christian traditions, teaches the redeeming nature of human suffering when it is joined with the crucified Jesus. This tradition goes back to the Apostle Paul's Letter to the Colossians: "I am now rejoicing in my sufferings for your sake, and in my flesh I am completing what is lacking in Christ's afflictions for the sake of his body, that is, the church" (1:24).

Try talking to Caryll. Feel free to pour out your heart to her as so many did to her during her life.

Blessings,
*Janice*

. . . . .

JANUARY 4, 2005

Dear Alexis,
Happy New Year! You asked for help with praying on days when you're feeling down. It's good to keep persisting in prayer even when it's tough to pray. God sees our desire and loves us for it even if we don't "feel" we're really praying.

Caryll Houselander clearly faced this dilemma herself, for she hits the nail on the head when she states that the place of the suffering of mental illness in the life of Jesus is his agony in the garden of Gethsemane. When praying about your own life situation, it can be helpful to find the place in the life of Christ that parallels it. For example, people with physical conditions can pray with Jesus during the Passion and crucifixion; they can turn to him and unite their pain with his, knowing his suffering was also acutely profound.

When you experience severe anxiety, deep depression, grieving or other forms of emotional distress, try praying with the anguished Jesus in *his* time of severe mental stress in Gethsemane. You can share your own emotional pain with him and know that he understands: When we pray, we can let the pain of our lives be the very thing to connect us to Jesus. This is not always easy, but it definitely makes the suffering we go through in life have meaning.

Blessings and prayers,
*Janice*

. . . . .

February 26, 2005

Dear Alex,
I've been reflecting a lot about your current prayer dilemma. I suggest a spiritual director—someone who can listen with the heart and who will help you keep your prayer organized and on track.

Also, I found some good advice in Caryll's letters, who definitely valued personal prayer and often gave advice about it in her correspondence. In one letter to a young friend who was dealing with an eating disorder, Caryll advised: "Let every meal be a prayer, every hour of sleep, every denial of an impulse to overdo things you feel a compulsion to—and believe me, you will at one and the same time cure yourself and cure the sufferings of the world."[20] It's hardly surprising that a woman with such profound love of God would dispense sound advice regarding prayer. Her own experience of mental illness makes her a wise spiritual adviser to others, *especially* to mentally ill people, who so often have difficulty focusing on traditional forms of prayer like meditation and contemplation.

Rather than stressing mental or verbal prayer, both of which require the ability to concentrate for a length of time, Caryll wisely advised her devoted correspondents of the value of the *prayer of intent:* "You should 'pray without ceasing'—*but,* not verbal prayer, not mental prayer, but the prayer of the body, and the prayer of acceptance and immolation. *Say* only one prayer a day; the morning offering of the Apostolate of Prayer is ideal: 'O my God, I offer you all my words, thoughts, actions and sufferings today, in union with your divine heart in the Holy Mass.'"[21] Wise spiritual advice for anyone—to offer one's *whole self*—every action, struggle, physical or emotional pain, indeed, every single breath to God. Then you are sure that you are in communion with God in every moment of every day. After a time you will become aware of a deepening intimacy with God, or "oneing" as Julian of Norwich called it.

Caryll's letter on prayer continues:

> Then let your prayer be simply your offering of yourself to do God's will, to *rest* and *relax* in Him, and to offer everything you *do* as a prayer, for example, if you have a little sleep, offer that; offer each mouthful of food that you eat, offer whatever you suffer, but all this simply and without any attempt at a formal offering in words, or any kind of meditation, or *thinking* about God.[22]

Like Thérèse of Lisieux, a saint for whom she had great respect, Caryll Houselander was aware of the tremendous spiritual power inherent in even the most mundane actions of daily life: "All that hidden daily suffering that seems insignificant will be redeeming the world, it will be healing the wounds of the world,"[23] Caryll tells us in *The Way of the Cross,* a wonderful book she both wrote and illustrated. When we are conscious of God's great love for us, then we know that the pains and joys we experience each day are cared about deeply. And Jesus smiles with joy when we give over our sufferings, both the great and the small, to be united with his for "healing the wounds of the world."

Caryll Houselander definitely had her share of suffering, dying at age fifty-three from breast cancer. Although she will probably never be canonized because she was so unconventional, her spirituality of inclusiveness and great love are desperately needed in our world today.

I must confess that I cried at the account of her death. After reading her letters and A Rocking Horse Catholic, I felt close to her.

When others insist on seeing my disability rather than the person I am, I know that Caryll understands. I have prayed with her spiritual advice often, imagining that she's writing or even speaking personally to me.

As hard as it is living with bipolar condition, I think you have a great advantage because you have a faith life. Keep inviting Jesus into your struggle and know he's always, always there for you.

I leave you with this final quote from Caryll: "It is love that redeems, love that can heal the world, love that can save it."[24] Good advice for all of us!

Many blessings,
*Janice*

. . . . .

## nine

CARDINAL JOSEPH BERNARDIN
*Our Companion in Cancer*
(1927–1996)

*I* am your brother Joseph."

These five simple words, uttered by Joseph Bernardin on his installation as archbishop of Chicago, say everything about this remarkable prelate's approach to life. Coming from the humblest of beginnings, and rising to the heights of the American Catholic hierarchy, Cardinal Bernardin made a profound impact on the Catholic church in America at the end of the twentieth century. His legacy is enormous: promulgating the doctrine of the "seamless garment," or consistent ethic of life; founding the still-flourishing Common Ground Initiative to bridge the gap between traditional and progressive Catholics; establishing guidelines for dioceses to consider regarding sexual abuse by priests. Joseph Bernardin was regarded as, above all, a unifier within the church.

As was characteristic, Cardinal Bernardin chose his five words well, deliberately using the reconciling words from Genesis 45 when

Joseph reveals his identity to his eleven brothers. Cardinal Bernardin was establishing a bond with the priests who would serve him as well as setting the tone for his tenure as archbishop of Chicago. Long known as a capable administrator and mediator, Joseph Bernardin also possessed enviable gifts for a cleric, being an unusually adept administrator with a genuine pastoral side.

As impressive as Cardinal Bernardin's career was, the impact of his spirituality on all Christians has been even more far-reaching. Events in his life taught him two lessons: the necessity of daily prayer and the importance of the interior spiritual disposition of letting go. Both became crucial in Joseph Bernardin's ability to deal serenely with the two most riveting events of his life: the false accusation of sexual abuse made against him and his two-year bout with pancreatic cancer. His most lasting legacy is without doubt *The Gift of Peace,* an account of these two major traumatic events of his life.

*Early Spirituality*

Growing up during the Depression in Eden, South Carolina, a small town in the rural South where his father worked quarrying marble, Cardinal Bernardin came from a very poor but very loving family. Losing his father to cancer at an early age plunged Joseph Bernardin's family (mother and younger sister) into near poverty. Although young, Joseph was up to the responsibilities placed on his shoulders. He learned to cook while his mother worked and consistently earned the highest grades throughout his school years. He earned a scholarship to the University of South Carolina, originally planning to become a doctor. However, after a conversation with young priests in his home parish, he changed his mind and entered the seminary for the Diocese of Charleston. He was ordained a priest in 1952 and served the Diocese of Charleston for fourteen years.

His obvious administrative gifts helped him to rise quickly in the church hierarchy. Ordained an auxiliary bishop for the Atlanta diocese in 1966, he was the youngest bishop in the country at the time. A scant two years later the newly formed National Conference of Catholic Bishops (NCCB) elected Bishop Bernardin its general secretary, an important and delicate post. Then, in 1972, Pope Paul VI appointed him archbishop of Cincinnati. During this time he also served as president of the NCCB. Pope John Paul II chose Archbishop Bernardin in 1982 for the see of Chicago, thereby elevating him to the College of Cardinals. In his book *The Gift of Peace*, Cardinal Bernardin later remembered fondly his tenure as archbishop of Chicago: "The past fourteen years in Chicago have been the most productive and blessed years of my life. It is here that I first began to articulate the need for a consistent ethic of life."[1] This "consistent ethic of life" or "seamless garment" calls Catholics to be consistent on life issues: to lobby against the death penalty as well as against abortion.

*Becoming a Pray-er*
In a candid section of *The Gift of Peace*, Cardinal Bernardin shares that not long after being made archbishop of Cincinnati, he began to feel hypocritical about exhorting others to pray when he was too busy to pray daily himself: "I was very busy, and I fell into the trap of thinking that my good works were more important than prayer."[2] He discussed his lack of a prayer life with three of his young priests over dinner one night: "In very direct—even blunt terms—they helped me realize that as a priest and a bishop I was urging a spirituality on others that I was not fully practicing myself. That was a turning point in my life."[3]

Archbishop Bernardin resolved to devote the first hour of his day, every day, to prayer and meditation. The fruit of his daily prayer was clear: "This put my life in a new and uplifting perspective; I also found that I was able to share the struggles of my own spiritual journey with others."[4] His long experience of spiritual sharing became crucial when he embarked on his final ministry with cancer patients.

*The Passion Begins*
Eugene Kennedy, a former priest and longtime friend of Cardinal Bernardin, wrote in his memoir *My Brother Joseph* that he received a

phone call from Cardinal Bernardin on November 11, 1993: "I've got something I have to talk to you about," Cardinal Bernardin said to his friend. "It appears that I am going to be named as a defendant in a sex-abuse case that will be filed tomorrow."[5] Kennedy had been hearing rumors that a high-ranking American prelate would be named in a sex scandal: "Nothing could be less possible and nothing could hurt him more than the public mugging of this sordid accusation."[6]

The next day the suit was filed in Ohio, stating that Cardinal Bernardin had sexually abused a man named Steven Cook while Steven had been a seminarian in Cincinnati. A media frenzy broke out, with cameras following the cardinal everywhere. Shortly before giving a press conference to defend himself, Cardinal Bernardin called Eugene to share his morning prayer with him: "It came clear to me.... I have to trust in God, who has allowed this for some purpose, and I have to put my trust in the truth. Jesus says in the Gospels that the truth will make us free. I believe that with all my heart."[7] In these days of public relations and spin control, the simple, unvarnished truth from a public leader is indeed a refreshing response to an accusation.

Cardinal Bernardin's years of praying to let go now stood him in good stead. The morning of the first of many press conferences he gave rebutting the charges against him, Cardinal Bernardin started the day with his usual hour of prayer. Reflecting on the First Sorrowful Mystery of the rosary, the Agony in the Garden, he prayed: "In all my sixty-five years, this is the first time I have really understood the pain and agony you felt that night." Cardinal Bernardin's personal spiritual depth allowed him to identify intimately with the suffering Jesus, even to the point of asking that perennially human question of God: "Why did you let this happen?"[8]

After meeting with his advisers, he again took an hour of quiet reflection and prayer to prepare himself to face the humiliating questions the reporters were sure to ask. "I was being emptied of self in a way that I never could have anticipated, and I wanted to let go and place myself and my cares in the hands of the Lord,"⁹ he wrote. Fortified by his prayer and his decision to defend himself with the simple truth that he had never abused anyone, Joseph Cardinal Bernardin went to meet the horde of reporters and their demanding, accusing questions.

*Moment of Grace*

Well aware that his forty-two years of priestly ministry and his reputation were on the line, Cardinal Bernardin's initial feeling as he stood before the microphones in front of him was one of profound loneliness. Yet at the same time he felt an inner strength that he knew could only come from the Lord. He also was aware of the spiritual opportunity that this ordeal presented: "For me, this moment of public accusation and inquiry was also a moment of grace...because I felt the great love and support that many people were giving me."¹⁰ Even at the darkest hour of his life, Cardinal Bernardin was able to turn the dross of human suffering into spiritual gold.

From the beginning, Cardinal Bernardin and his friends suspected that this sordid accusation was part of a conspiracy to bring him down: "I was angry and bewildered that people who did not know me would make such destructive charges against me. There seemed to be some calculation involved because these accusations could not be construed as some innocent misunderstanding of facts."¹¹ Indeed, many of Cardinal Bernardin's friends were convinced that the accusation was part of a conspiracy to smear his good name.

*Vindication*

Cardinal Bernardin gave fourteen press conferences during the next week. Slowly, the truth became known: There was absolutely no evidence of any kind against him. At the end of February 1994, three months after the filing of the lawsuit, Steven Cook, of his own initiative, recanted the charges he had made against the cardinal of Chicago and dropped the suit. Though his lawyers asked him to consider a counter lawsuit, Cardinal Bernardin chose not to, as he did not want to discourage people who had really suffered abuse from coming forward. Reflecting on this period in his life, Cardinal Bernardin termed it an "education of the soul."[12]

## Reconciliation

Although fully exonerated and now able to concentrate once more on his pastoral duties as head of the American church's second-largest see, Cardinal Bernardin remained troubled by one aspect of his ordeal: the plight of his accuser, Steven Cook. Once a seminarian, Cook had since contracted AIDS and was being cared for by a friend in an apartment in Philadelphia. Realizing all along that Cook had been a pawn of his reactionary critics, Cardinal Bernardin felt genuine compassion: "I thought often of Steven in his lonely, illness-ridden exile from both his parental home and the Church."[13] Joseph Bernardin felt a strong need to reconcile in person with Cook in order to bring the whole episode to closure.

Accordingly, in December 1994, Cardinal Bernardin met with Steven Cook and his friend at St. Charles Seminary in Philadelphia. Cook apologized for the false accusation. Cardinal Bernardin then celebrated Mass for him and the two parted on good terms.

Buoyed by his reconciliation with Cook, Cardinal Bernardin not only now felt that he had a new lease on life, but he also experienced the spiritual strength that flows from genuinely forgiving another. He traveled to several different countries to lecture and also visited the Holy Land, where he resolved he would return one day to pray in private. His gratitude to God for his total vindication was profound.

## The Passion Continues: Cancer

Sadly, while Joseph Bernardin basked in the light of his renewed life, a sinister shadow was lurking in his body. In June of 1995 his physicians diagnosed the sixty-seven-year-old cardinal with pancreatic cancer, which is nearly always fatal. After the humiliating public suffering he had just been through, it would have been understandable for him to focus only on his own healing and keep the pain of others at a distance. Instead, he fought against the very human tendency to withdraw into himself that many people with serious illness experience. "When we are ill, we tend to focus on our own pain and suffering. We may feel sorry for ourselves or become depressed."[14] Certainly, a period of depression and grieving is to be expected after being diagnosed with a serious illness. Sometimes it may be necessary to seek out a counselor or spiritual director for support. The love of family and friends is also critical. Possibly the most important thing, however, is to place ourselves and our illness in the light of God and pray with the illness itself, allowing it to hollow out our being to make greater room there for Jesus.

For Joseph Bernardin, it was again necessary to dig deep into his soul for the spiritual strength that had sustained him throughout the ordeal of being falsely accused. Once again, he drew on his deep faith: "Suffering and pain make little sense to me without God, and my heart goes out to people who feel abandoned or alone in their greatest times of need."[15] To him, suffering was above all an invitation. His call was to embrace his pain squarely, to find God in it.

Cardinal Bernardin decided to share his life with cancer with the public, not to elicit sympathy, but to send others with cancer or serious illness the signal that a time of illness is precisely *not* the time to close in on ourselves. Cardinal Bernardin soon also realized, however, that he was "a priest first, a patient second"[16] and became intensely involved in ministering to his fellow cancer patients.

Because they knew he suffered as they did, people with cancer from all around the world were contacting him to offer prayer and ask for prayer in return. According to *My Brother Joseph*: "Other cancer patients spontaneously sought him out—please pray for me, my mother, my husband, my cousin. The prayer list finally exceeded six hundred, and Joseph spent a great deal of time answering letters from cancer patients, calling them on the phone or visiting them, particularly the children, in the hospital."[17] At public events, many came up to him just to touch him, spontaneously expressing their conviction that here was a genuinely holy man, someone they could lean on. The press dubbed him the "unofficial chaplain" of persons dealing with cancer.

*Physical Pain*

Cardinal Bernardin embarked on the usual treatment for serious cases of cancer: surgery, chemotherapy and radiation. After a lengthy surgery that removed the cancer cells from his pancreas, Cardinal Bernardin underwent the typical pancreatic cancer therapy: six weeks of radiation, accompanied by chemotherapy. In addition, the doctors diagnosed him with spinal stenosis, a painful condition in which the bones of the spine shrink, causing severe pain. Also, after a series of falls, he was diagnosed with osteoporosis, which eventually caused him to lose four inches of height. Physical pain became his constant companion.

After a particularly painful fall on steps in January 1996, Cardinal Bernardin was required to stay in bed while the fracture in his spine healed. His friend Eugene Kennedy notes the parallels to the Passion of Christ: "Joseph, like Jesus on the *via crucis*, had fallen the first time. Joseph had been called, at the time I thought he would be pope, to live out a Passion Play of Gospel values, of faith and suffering that was redeeming the rest of us."[18]

*God's Special Gift*

It is my personal belief that God showers us with goodness and graces every day. We must do our part, however, and open ourselves to receive these gifts. Joseph Bernardin had prayed for the grace of letting go—of letting *nothing* come between him and Jesus. That grace had been sorely tested when he was falsely accused of sexual abuse. However, his years of prayer bore fruit. He knew, in the midst of the firestorm of accusations and vilifications, that Jesus was always with him.

The same was true of his initial cancer diagnosis. His lifelong prayer of letting go of all that was not of Jesus steadied and strengthened him throughout surgery, pain, chemotherapy and radiation. In a pastoral letter on Catholic health care issued in October 1995, Cardinal Bernardin shared how he dealt with his own struggle with cancer: "I determined that I would offer whatever suffering I might endure for the Church, particularly the Archdiocese of Chicago. Blessedly, a peace of mind and heart and soul quietly flooded through my entire being, a kind of peace I had never known before."[19]

Cardinal Bernardin was aware of this particular grace that God offered to him: the gift of peace: "God's special gift to me has been the ability to accept difficult situations, especially the false accusation made against me and then the cancer. His special gift to me is the gift of peace. In turn, my special gift to others is to share God's peace, to help them deal with illness, troubled times."[20]

It is understandable that the grace of peace comes after a person has truly been able to let go and focus totally on God. We are able to place our usual cares and concerns—jobs, finances, even beloved family and friends—in a different perspective and trust that God will take care of what needs tending to.

*Cancer Returns*
When Cardinal Bernardin was initially diagnosed with cancer of the pancreas, his physicians told him he had one chance in four of living five more years. In August of 1996, one year after his initial diagnosis, his doctor said the word that every person with cancer dreads the most: recurrence. The cancer had spread to his liver. His doctor told him he had one year to live.

Despite the consistently prayerful approach he had taken his whole life, Cardinal Bernardin was still human and was devastated by this news. Eugene Kennedy describes his response: "He was not self-pitying, nor was he a stoic. He felt the weight of his illness, this enemy within, wily and watchful, that, like a thief who knew when you were off guard, had come out of hiding—for he had never really gone; Joseph never was 'cancer free.'"[21]

Joseph Bernardin began to prepare for his own death: notifying the Vatican, shoring up his projects, searching for a coadjutor bishop to begin assisting in administering the archdiocese of Chicago.

## Joseph Bernardin as Companion

The spiritual legacy of Cardinal Joseph Bernardin rests squarely on consistent prayer. In prayer he sought the grace of letting go, which supported him through the trial of false accusation. The grace of letting go became utterly crucial after his diagnosis with cancer. It permitted him to eventually let go *even of his own life* and view death not as an enemy, but as a friend.

## Daily Prayer

As busy as he was, Cardinal Bernardin was faithful to his promise to God; he always devoted the first hour of his day to prayer. Being human, he experienced distractions and at times was problem-solving in his head rather than praying. But he persisted, telling Jesus that this was sacred time devoted to God alone. The fruit of his prayer became clear: "That hour certainly unites me with the Lord in the early part of the day, but it keeps me connected to him throughout the rest of the day as well."[22]

Connecting to God, knowing Jesus is with us—this is what prayer is all about. Jesus is always beckoning; it is up to us to respond by giving the time and effort that prayer requires. Whatever hour of the day, it is important for us to pray consistently. For people who are ill, a prayer life is especially crucial. It is our prayer that blesses the physical devastation of illness and disability and transforms it, uniting us with God. Prayer helps us, strengthens us and brings us ever closer to Jesus. We may have little control over what is happening to our bodies, but we can choose to turn our souls to Jesus. We may live with physical pain, but we can unite it with the sacred stream that flows from Jesus' side. We may lack the concerted energy for a full hour of meditative prayer, but we can use other means: repeating the name of Jesus over and over, gazing at a holy picture, playing religious music and letting the words pray for us. What is important is to turn our being to God *in any way we can* and let God do the rest.

*Letting Go*

*The Gift of Peace,* written in the last weeks of Joseph Bernardin's life, opens with a chapter titled "Letting Go." Asking Jesus for the grace of letting go was the foundation of Cardinal Bernardin's prayer life, and it helped prepare him spiritually for the ordeals of false accusation and terminal cancer.

What exactly is "letting go"? Why is it important for us to try to relinquish our desire to control other people, to manipulate situations, to make everything come out the way *we* want? It is certainly human to think we know what is best for ourselves, or for our family and friends. Most of us, however, have also had the experience of looking back on a situation and realizing that God worked things out far better than we would have planned ourselves.

The concept of "letting go" is a simple but important one in the spiritual life. Ignatius of Loyola gave us the idea of "indifference," or detachment from anything that hinders our lives in God, in his famous prayer "The Principle and Foundation" at the beginning of *The Spiritual Exercises.* John of the Cross, Teresa of Avila—many of the great spiritual teachers of the Christian tradition—have emphasized the importance of not becoming too attached to anything that keeps us from God. Even today in Twelve Step programs, this spiritual wisdom has been distilled into the simple yet profound expression: "Let go and let God."

We can invite our brother Joseph to teach us about detachment: "By letting go, I mean the ability to release from our grasp those things that inhibit us from developing an intimate relationship with the Lord Jesus…. But letting go is possible if we understand the importance of opening our hearts and, above all else, developing a healthy prayer life."[23] It is certainly not easy to winnow out of our lives all that does not lead to God alone. Our responsibilities, power, status and material possessions can block the face of God from us if we let them. It takes energy and effort to keep our focus on God and hold earthly possessions lightly in our hands.

Next to daily prayer, the interior disposition of letting go is crucial when living with serious illness. Through our prayer, we ask continually for the grace to put ourselves in the hands of Jesus. This does not mean we become passive and uncaring about our lives. Rather, we live our lives as before, but without clinging to ideas of the results *we* desire in situations, especially situations over which we have little control. God so often brings about far better results than we could have wished for anyway. When we let go of our own will, it makes more room in our souls for the activity of God.

*Befriending Death*

Our youth-idolizing culture has a horror of death. We are even presumptuous enough to attempt to defy the aging process with hair dye, wrinkle creams and tummy tucks. Certainly, it is human to fear the unknown. No one welcomes the dying process. It is vital, however, to view death through the lens of faith, which assures us that death is a transition to life eternal. The funeral liturgy states clearly that "life is changed, not ended."

After a conversation with his good friend Henri Nouwen, Cardinal Bernardin began to view death with a different attitude. The key was to continually turn to Jesus and simply let go. For as Nouwen instructed him: "If we let go of ourselves—and our own resources— and allow the Lord to help us, we will be able to see death not as an enemy or a threat but as a friend."[24]

*Requiescat*

Joseph Bernardin met his "friend" death in the early morning hours of November 14, 1996. Pastor to the end, he worked hard to finish *The*

*Gift of Peace,* the best-selling account of the false accusations against him and his journey with cancer. The first copy was placed in his lap on the day he died. He was eager to share what God had taught him: "What I would like to leave behind is a simple prayer that each of you may find what I have found—God's special gift to us all: the gift of peace. When we are at peace, we find the freedom to be most fully who we are, even in the worst of times. We let go of what is nonessential and embrace what is essential. We empty ourselves so that God may more fully work within us. And we become instruments in the hands of the Lord."[25]

Yes, this is easier said than done. Easing our fear of death is a tremendous spiritual challenge. Perhaps how we view death reflects the depth of our faith. Do we really believe in eternal life? Do we know in our hearts that our God loves us intimately and will welcome our coming home with open arms? Cardinal Joseph Bernardin's legacy to us is to turn conventional wisdom on its head and welcome death when our time arrives. He invites us to befriend death and thus lessen its grip of fear over us. His years of praying to let go of what *he* wanted allowed more room in his soul for God. This strengthened him when he was most in need of detachment in his life. Eventually this continual prayer for the grace of detachment permitted him to let go of *even his own life.*

The annals of the Catholic church in America will record for posterity the many achievements of this unusually gifted cardinal. In particular, he will be remembered for his efforts to reconcile a fractious church. The annals of American spirituality, however, will revere Cardinal Bernardin for a greater achievement: allowing Jesus to teach him to let go of his own life in order to embrace his own death. In doing this, our brother Joseph received the finest gift of all, the legacy he yearns to leave each one of us: the gift of peace.

Forever.

ten

SISTER THEA BOWMAN
*Our Companion in Joy-Filled Suffering*
(1937–1990)

he first thing one notices about the bald woman in African dress sitting upright in her wheelchair is how strikingly beautiful she is. Her brown eyes look searchingly into the camera with a look both compassionate and intelligent. Yet it is her smile that totally captivates—a broad smile, a smile that tells the viewer that this is indeed a woman wrapped in perpetual joy.

She is Sister Thea Bowman, Franciscan Sister of Perpetual Adoration (FSPA), granddaughter of a slave and a prominent teacher, activist and advocate for black Catholics in America.

And she is dying from cancer.

In the video *Almost Home: Living with Suffering and Dying*, Sister Thea Bowman makes one thing perfectly clear: "I intend to live until I die."[1] Thea relates with grace and dignity her thoughts and feelings as she journeys home to the God she loves. Ever the teacher, Thea invites us to contemplate death as "part of the cycle of reality that is part of

God's plan."[2] The greatest lesson, the greatest gift Sister Thea Bowman has to give each of us is her example of courage and faith-filled joy in the face of approaching death.

*Early Years*

Bertha Bowman, born in 1937 to Theon Bowman, a physician, and Mary Esther Coleman, a teacher, grew up in the small Mississippi town of Canton. An only child, she said of herself: "I was what people called an 'old folks' child.' My parents were older, and I spent a lot of time around their friends who were grandparents and great grandparents. They made a deliberate effort to teach me about life."[3] Canton, Mississippi, was a poor town with segregated neighborhoods. Distressed that her daughter was not able to read after five years in the public school, Esther Bowman transferred her to the local Catholic school, staffed by the Franciscan Sisters of Perpetual Adoration. Young Bertha flourished in her new, challenging educational environment, cherishing the fact that the Franciscans both challenged and cared for their students.

Bertha Bowman came from a rich, ecumenical faith background: Her father was an Episcopalian, her mother a Methodist. She was drawn to Catholicism, however, and received the sacrament of baptism in 1947. At age sixteen Bertha felt God calling her to a religious vocation: "I wanted to be part of the effort to help feed the hungry, find shelter for the homeless, and teach the children."[4] Her pastor, Father Justin Fuhrman, advised her to join the Holy Family Community of Black Sisters in New Orleans. Bertha, however, knew she was called to join the women who had made such a difference in her life—the Franciscan Sisters of Perpetual Adoration, based in La Crosse, Wisconsin.

Although her father warned her that being the only black woman in the convent would be challenging and that the white people might not like her, Bertha knew she was hearing God's voice. "I felt that God had called me and if he didn't want me there he'd send me home," she said.[5] She entered the Franciscan Sisters of Perpetual Adoration in 1953, choosing "Thea" ("of God") as her religious name in honor of her father, Theon.

Having an African-American as a fellow aspirant was a cultural experience for the white sisters who were with Thea in formation. One of them, Sister Marla Lang, explained, "Most of us were from Wisconsin farms and urban areas. I had never had an opportunity to speak to an African-American before, so there was a certain intrigue for us to hear from her about her culture and her experience of life."[6] She and the other young sisters were also amazed by Thea's love of singing: "Whenever we'd ask her, she would love to sing. This was really an eye opener for us because most sixteen-year-olds when asked to sing claim they can't, but Thea always said 'Sure.' One of the songs she loved to sing was 'Little David, Play on Your Harp.' A vivid memory I have of her was her absolute joy at being asked to sing," continued Sister Marla.[7]

*Pass the Posies*

Another classmate of Thea's, Sister Jean Kasparbauer, reflects on her friendship with Thea dating from their early days in formation: "At the time, I had no idea of the struggle that Thea was going through in a 'white' world. I knew we were all adjusting and did not suspect that her struggle included not only adjustment to convent life but also living without her kind of food, her kind of music, her kind of prayer, her kind of flexibility. Her adjustment meant that she lived in a cold, northern, highly organized environment."[8] Thea, exhibiting the resiliency of spirit that she would later call on again when coping with cancer, started a custom with her classmates that she called "Pass the Posies." While they were all present during recreation time, each would share something good that she had heard about another member of their class. This was a much needed experience of affirmation for young women finding their way in religious life: "I am sure," says Sister Jean, "that this custom of ours contributed greatly to our sense of belonging and community."[9]

Sister Thea, like many in her formation class, studied for her undergraduate degree at her community's college, Viterbo College, in La Crosse, Wisconsin. Thea loved her time there, but found some aspects difficult: "It was a lonely experience for me culturally, because very little of what I studied pertained to my past, my experience, the contributions of my people."[10] Armed with her Bachelor of Arts degree, Sister Thea taught elementary school for a few years, then returned to her hometown of Canton to teach English and vocal music at Holy Child Jesus Catholic High School. As a teacher, Thea had high expectations for her students and taught them to be proud to be black and Catholic. "Always remember who you are and Whose you are," she frequently reminded her young students.[11] After ten years of teaching, her community asked her to study at Catholic University so that she could return to teach at Viterbo.

### Being Black and Catholic

Thea's time at Catholic University was a major turning point in her life. Sister Patricia Alden comments, "I think that it may have been in her stay at Catholic University that it was the first time that Sister Thea really became aware of her blackness and could say of herself: I'm black and I'm beautiful; and I love myself."[12]

At Catholic University Thea met and socialized for the first time with other African-American religious and priests. She began to think deeply about what it really meant to be black and Catholic, about the free expression of black Catholic worship, and about black spirituality itself—its participatory, affirming nature. After being invited to give a presentation at Catholic University on the oral tradition of black people, Thea started giving the talk on the D.C. college circuit. These presentations were the beginning of her remarkable career on the national Catholic level, teaching the depth and importance of African-American spirituality.

### "Everybody is so pale here"

Back at Viterbo College, Thea taught English, eventually becoming chair of the English Department. Evidencing the joy that was so characteristic of her, Thea said: "One of my primary objectives was that I should have a good time, that my students should have a good time and enjoy what we were doing."[13] After her years at Catholic University, she had a broader, deeper perspective on herself and her people. She also realized more than ever how crucial diversity is: "Everybody is so pale here," she would remark occasionally to her friend and colleague Sister Charlene Smith.[14]

Thea Bowman was a master teacher who had the ability not only to impart knowledge, but to do much more—to touch her students' hearts and souls. She was famous for encouraging her students to think for themselves, to be themselves, to love themselves. She both challenged and supported at the same time: "She did push you to the edge, and it was simply to let you know you can fly, but she also let you know that if your wings are not ready yet, she'd be there to catch you when you fall," says former student Sister Eva Marie Lumas.[15]

A beautiful story that illustrates Thea's role as nurturer and mentor, in addition to teacher, took place with Father Maurice Nutt, whose mother had just died. Thea and her class were discussing death and the communion of saints when Father Maurice broke down and wept openly. Thea came to him and, putting her arms around him, consoled him by humming and swaying, just as his mother used to do. Thea used this "teachable moment" to show Father Maurice and the other students that he was not a motherless child, that he had friends and a community to nurture and support him.[16]

Thea taught at Viterbo College for six years, then returned to Mississippi in 1978 to care for her parents, who were by now growing frail. During this time the bishop of the Diocese of Jackson, Mississippi, asked her to serve as consultant and eventually director of the Office for Intercultural Awareness. She soon became a much sought-after speaker at national Catholic events, focusing on integrating African-American spirituality into Catholicism in America.

*Multi-Culturalism: Bridge Over Troubled Waters*
Segregation had legally ended in the United States. However, since it is far easier to pass laws than to change hearts, racism remained very much alive in America, even within the Catholic church. Thea Bowman brought her unique gifts and background into this setting, challenging society and the church to become more multicultural. She strongly believed that her call was to integrate African-American spirituality into the Catholic church in America, to be a "bridge over troubled waters." She didn't stop at black spirituality, however. Thea wanted *all* people to come together at God's table: "I can introduce my black friends to my Hispanic friends, to my Anglo friends, to my Asian friends, to my native friends. I can be a bridge over troubled waters. I can take you by the hand and take you with me into the black community. I can walk with you into your community. And if I walk with you into your community, I don't walk as a stranger, I walk as your sister."[17]

Bringing that rich diversity into her church was Thea Bowman's mission: "From the Bishops to the children, from the white collar to the no collar, from the United States to the shores of Africa, Thea challenged, debated and evangelized the same message: 'We are all God's children and there is room for all of us.'"[18] Thea used every one of her God-given gifts to get across her message of total inclusiveness. A presentation by Sister Thea Bowman wasn't just a presentation—it was a total multicultural experience that was unforgettable. Thea sang spirituals in her beautiful soprano voice, wore African dress, danced all over the stage, slipped into "black folks" dialect from time to time as she informed, challenged and invited her audience to grow.

*The Diagnosis*
Then came March 1984. After discovering a lump on her breast, Thea received the diagnosis that every woman dreads: breast cancer.

"I thought it was a mistake at first," says Thea's close friend Sister Dorothy Kundinger, "since Thea's mother was also in the hospital at the time, I thought that they had the wrong Bowman. I didn't really believe it until I went in and saw her all bandaged up in the bed."[19] Unfortunately, it was the right person: Thea's initial prognosis was that she would only have a few months, at most a year or two, left to live. She underwent a mastectomy and started a regimen of radiation and chemotherapy.

After dealing with the normal fears and depression that one typically experiences upon hearing the diagnosis of cancer, Thea responded in typical Thea Bowman style: She resolved to keep on keeping on. The deep reservoir of faith resulting from the years spent with the elders of Canton, her many years of personal prayer as a Franciscan, the fortitude she derived from her knowledge of the strength of her African ancestors—all combined to enable Thea to continue her ministry of incorporating African-American spirituality into the Catholic church.

At times, Thea's resolve to "live until I die" cost her a great deal. Anyone who has experienced the debilitating effects of chemotherapy and radiation knows how difficult it must have been for Thea to continue her ministry of teaching, writing and speaking at national events, no matter how unwell she felt.

Although radiation and chemotherapy usually help to shrink tumors, they also have a harsh effect on the body: The immune system becomes suppressed, making the person susceptible to infection, including mouth lesions and other sores. Chemotherapy kills the fast-growing cancer cells, but it also kills the body's normal fast-growing cells, resulting in hair loss. Above all, the chemo-radiation regimen is extremely wearing, causing a great deal of fatigue. In deadly cancers, the chemo eventually stops working and the tumors win.

*Weeping Bishops*
"Electrifying!" That's how one bishop described Sister Thea Bowman's June 1989 presentation to the United States Catholic Conference of Bishops at Seton Hall University in South Orange,

New Jersey. In many ways, Thea's presentation was the culmination of her call as a prophet and advocate for African-Americans in the Catholic church. Thea, using her wheelchair and wearing African dress, challenged and exhorted the bishops to be inclusive of African-Americans in the church and to be leaders in reaching out to marginalized people all over the earth.

"She began by singing 'Sometimes I feel like a motherless child / A long way from home.'"[20] After asking the bishops, "What does it mean to be black in these United States?" she eloquently summarized the history and contributions of African-Americans. Then, hitting closer to home, Thea asked: "What does it mean to be black and Catholic?... I bring myself, my black self, all that I am, all that I have, all that I hope to become, I bring my whole history, my traditions, my experience, my culture, my African-American song and dance and gesture and movement and teaching and preaching and healing and responsibility as gift to the church."[21]

Thea continued with a beautiful summary of African-American spirituality: "I bring...a spirituality [that] is contemplative and biblical and holistic, bringing to religion a totality of minds and imagination, of memory, of feeling and passion and emotion and intensity, of faith that is embodied, incarnate praise...a spirituality that is communal, that tries to walk and talk and work and pray and play together—even with the bishops."[22]

As she concluded, Thea did an amazing thing: She invited the bishops to stand with a "C'mon, y'all get up!" She then burst into the anthem of the civil rights movement: "We Shall Overcome" and invited the bishops of the United States not only to sing along, but to join hands with one another. It was quite an astonishing sight: More than two hundred American bishops on their feet, many with tears in their eyes, hands clasped with one another, swaying together singing: "We Shall Overcome."

Thea concluded by directly challenging the bishops. Speaking of the civil rights marches, she reminded them that they and the church clergy were in the front where they should actually *lead* the people. When she finished, bishops stood in line to meet her and talk with her. In the background, Thea's companion, Sister Dorothy, waited patiently.

*"Dort"*

Wherever Thea is, she's there. At conferences, on the videotapes, in the books about Thea Bowman, one will find Sister Dorothy Ann Kundinger. It began in 1979, when Thea, living with and caring for her parents, called the nearby FSPA convent and asked if anyone would like to accompany her on weekend road trips. Sister Dorothy, teaching at Holy Child, the same elementary school Thea had attended, saw this as an opportunity to learn more about Mississippi and agreed to go along. From these road trips a deep and lasting friendship grew.

In 1984, just as Thea learned her own devastating diagnosis and while her parents were also in need of care, Dorothy moved into the Bowman home to help Thea care for them. As Thea and Dorothy grew closer, Thea often referred to her friend by her family nickname, "Dort."

Thea said of her good friend: "She has borne the frustration, she's helped me bear the pain, she's just been there. I think sometimes people don't realize how much strength, how much help, how much support a person who is ill can derive just by the presence of somebody who loves, somebody who cares, somebody who understands."[23]

Mutuality in relationship at every level, from personal to institutional, was extremely important to Thea. As so many people who have accompanied a loved one during serious illness or death have discovered, one receives as much as one gives in this Jesus-based exchange of love. The caregiver's attitude, of course, is crucial. Sister Dorothy is aware of this when she says, "The blessings of the friendship go both ways. I'm the one who's blessed. I'm the one that's honored that in my lifetime I could walk with somebody as they went home. Also, I was blessed because I got to meet a community much larger than myself, I got to meet persons who loved Thea and I could see their interactions with her and her interactions with them, how she grew and how they grew."[24]

*Sacrament*

Perhaps the hardest part of any illness or disability is being dependent on others for the basic necessities of life. We cannot help but feel we are letting down others in that subtle but real human dynamic that says everyone contributes, everyone pulls her or his weight in relationships. A society that worships independence makes things even worse. If one has lived for many years barely giving a passing thought to life's basic necessities, suddenly having to depend on others is truly difficult. The gospel of Jesus Christ, however, says not a word about being totally self-sufficient. Rather, the invitation is clear: Love and care for one another.

As with so many other aspects of illness and disability, grace can flow freely through this dynamic of human interdependence. Certainly, being a humble receiver of assistance or care is difficult, but it helps to remember that there was no one more vulnerable or needy than Jesus hanging on the cross. And he permitted others to minister to him: Simon of Cyrene carrying his cross, his mother and the other women silently exercising a ministry of presence at the foot of his cross as he died.

When we have the grace to realize the love that lies behind the caregiving, it can be a bit easier to humbly accept the assistance. As we have seen with Catherine of Genoa, the whole caregiving dynamic is an exchange of love—in a sense, a sacrament, a witness to others that God is alive every day: care freely offered and lovingly received.

Thea Bowman realized that in order to "live until I die," she needed personal assistance. She and her friend Sister Dorothy are beautiful models of the sacramental exchange of love. Thea was grateful for Dorothy's presence, her caregiving, her support. Dorothy remains aware that the blessings in their sacred exchange of love were mutual.

Both of Thea's parents died in 1984. Despite her grief and her own physical situation, Thea kept up a busy schedule of speaking engagements. Dorothy, feeling it was time to move from teaching to another ministry, accompanied her everywhere, loading her wheelchair into the trunk of the car, administering medicines and generally ministering to Thea as they traveled around the United States.

In 1989 it became necessary for Thea to use a wheelchair, as the bones in her back were weakening. As determined as ever, Thea persisted in her ministry, often bringing her chemotherapy medicines along on her travels. No matter how ill she was, Thea was resolved not to miss any speaking engagements.

By that summer, Thea was beginning to weaken. In August of that year, Thea's formation classmates had a reunion at their motherhouse in Wisconsin. Since Thea was too ill to attend, they decided to phone her in Mississippi. Sister Marla remembers well their conversation: "Marla," Thea asked, "do you think my life and my ministry have made any difference at all?" Caught off guard, Marla realized that Thea was reviewing her life in ministry and its effectiveness. "All those years she spent crisscrossing that country and beyond, speaking to hundreds of thousands of people, tending to a part of the church that needed to unfold more fully, begging for the empowerment of her people, and she was so effective in that. Yet in this moment of illness she questioned that. To me it said she didn't fully realize how the impact of, she really lit up the church in the U.S. by her overflowing of affection for all in it."[25]

*Live Until I Die*

We are blessed to have the videotape *Almost Home: Living with Suffering and Dying,* because it captures the energy and dynamism of Sister Thea Bowman as words on a page simply cannot. Self-giving to the end,

Thea permits the viewer to accompany her on the most intimate journey in life—the dying process. Thea is honest about her feelings, her fears and her faith, and she speaks openly about her experiences and thoughts: "I think that cancer causes one to reevaluate priorities, to have some very different perceptions of what's important in life and what's not important in life. I have a different sense of time and its importance. All my relationships, including my relationship to God, are more important to me too."[26]

These words ring loudly and clearly to those of us who live with significant illness or disability. When we have limited energy, and hence limited time, we realize God's invitation to focus on the truly important things in life. When living with intractable pain, or using oxygen to facilitate breathing, or slowly losing the ability to see, we have a choice: We can continually mourn our lost self, or we can focus on the good things we still have, especially, as Thea points out, our relationships with others. Sometimes it's hard to tell our family and friends just how much they mean to us. A subtle grace of illness can be the freedom of opening up about our deepest feelings to the dearest people in our lives. Toward the end of *Almost Home*, Thea says, "I find myself much more willing, much more eager to tell people that I love them. I find myself much more eager to tell them what they mean in my life."[27]

Just as she used her God-given gifts in her ministry, Thea used them again to help her cope when she was unwell. Singing made her feel better, as did a practice she had learned from the old folks around whom she had grown up—moaning. "Sometimes other people hear you moaning and they get upset. But the old folks, they would just moan. Sometimes as children we would imitate them and laugh. But as you get older, you find out it works."[28] Thea elaborated on how moaning helped her: "I've found that moaning is therapeutic. It's a way of centering, the way you do in centering prayer. You concentrate your internal energies and your powers in prayer or wordless outcry to

God."[29] Although practices like moaning can be a bit disconcerting to loved ones, grief counselors stress the importance of "getting it out," of expressing physical pain and hard emotions, whether by talking or writing them out; drawing or sketching; singing, humming or moaning; or, most importantly, pouring out one's heart to God.

In *Almost Home* Thea is honest about her prayer during the days immediately following her diagnosis: "At first, I didn't know what to pray for. Then I began to pray to live until I die...what I say is I want to live *fully*, I want to love fully, I want to give fully. I want to be the best person that I can during the time that I have."[30]

Live fully she certainly did, doing her best to meet every commitment, no matter the cost: "I am making a conscious effort to learn to live with discomfort, and, at the same time, to go about my work. I find that when I am involved in the business of life, when I'm working with people, particularly with children, I feel better. A kind of strength and energy comes with that."[31] Again, Thea falls back on African-American styles of prayer: "Our prayer tradition attempts to go to God with feeling and passion and emotion and intensity. I want to be a part of what Jesus felt as he hung on the cross. I want to feel the anguish. I want to feel the love that motivated him to save us."[32]

Wanting to feel the anguish and the love of Jesus, not unlike Julian of Norwich's deepest desire—what a beautiful way to show one's love!

*Salve Regina*
On Tuesday, March 27, 1990, shortly before her death, Thea Bowman went to her oncologist for a routine visit. The following day she became quite ill and unresponsive. As word spread to her many friends around the country that she was failing, the phone began to ring. Dorothy held the phone to Thea's ear as she managed to speak. On Thursday, she rallied slightly. Her close friend, Father John Ford, gave her a simple yet profound piece of advice: "Don't be afraid." Thea listened, says Dorothy: "I don't know what those touching words

meant to her, but she really relaxed and took them to heart. From then on, she wasn't afraid."[33]

That evening, two friends, Father Bede Abrams and Brother Thaddeus Posey, came to see Thea. As they sat with her, they sang the "Salve Regina," the hymn their community sings when brothers are dying. Their presence, as well as the majestic Latin of the ancient hymn about Mary, also had a calming effect on Thea.

On Friday, March 30, 1990, Sister Thea Bowman went home to the Jesus whom she had loved and served ardently her entire life.

*Legacy*

Although Thea Bowman now rests in the arms of Jesus, her spirit lives on in the hearts of all who knew and loved her: in the Catholic church, particularly the African-American Catholic church, and in her religious community, which is doing a great deal to keep her memory alive through the Internet, commemorative gatherings and a newsletter. Since her death, more and more people have come to know and love Thea. A simple Internet search yields at least sixty organizations and schools named after her. The Thea Bowman Foundation grants scholarships. There is a growing body of Thea literature. Many speak of canonization.

Thea Bowman's mission in the Catholic church focused on it being inclusive of *all*. This alone makes her a powerful intercessor for people with physical and mental disabilities, as well as those who live on the margins of society. We can, however, turn to Thea for much more. We can turn to her for spiritual friendship, especially when we are not feeling well but are wanting and needing to continue with our lives. That's the exact moment one should send a prayer to Thea Bowman and listen for her joy-filled, courageous response: "Keep on keeping on."

In the year before she died, Thea gave interviews to several Catholic periodicals. In response to a question about her image of God, she replied:

My people graced me with multiple images of the living God. God is bread when you're hungry, water when you're thirsty, a harbor from the storm. God's a father to the fatherless, a mother to the motherless. God's my sister, my brother, my leader, my guide, my teacher, my comforter, my friend. God's the way-maker and burden-bearer, a heart-fixer and a mind-regulator. God's my doctor who never lost a patient, my lawyer who never lost a case, my chaplain who never lost a battle. God's my all in all, my everything.[34]

And God is Sister Thea Bowman's ol' folks child ing, "uf-God-ing," *always* teaching, what-it-means-to-be-black and-Catholic-ing, national-Catholic-circuit-speaking, black spiritual-singing, inviting-the-bishops-to-dancing, therapeutic-moaning, almost-homing, keep-on-keeping-on-ing, seams-bursting with joy-ing, Sister Thea Bowman.

Thea, please teach us how to live until we die.

## eleven

FATHER PEDRO ARRUPE
*Our Companion in Stroke*
(1907–1991)

*H*e was sitting quietly in his study, talking with another Jesuit when it happened. A blinding flash of light followed by a huge explosion threw him and his companion from their room and into the hall.

It was August 6, 1945, and Father Pedro Arrupe was performing his duties as Novice Master in the Japanese town of Nagatsuka, when the atomic bomb fell on Hiroshima. This was one of the foundational life experiences that prepared Father Arrupe not only for his eventual tenure as Superior General of the Society of Jesus, but also for the ten years of silent and struggling daily living resulting from a severe cerebral thrombosis.

Pedro Arrupe was a man of the twentieth century. He witnessed firsthand its horrors of Nazism and atomic bombing, as well as the benefits of antibiotic therapy and the fall of Communism. As he had been elected Superior General of the Jesuits in the midst of the

Second Vatican Council, he attended the Council's final session, helping to shape one of its most famous documents, the *Gaudium et Spes*
(Pastoral Constitution on the Church in the Modern World). He
lived in many parts of the world: Spain, Holland, the United States,
Japan and Italy. In the time-honored tradition of Jesuit Superior
Generals, Father Arrupe was devoted to the papacy: "Moved by an
intense, lifelong fidelity to the church and a deep personal loyalty to
the Holy Father, he became a major commentator on and promoter of
the decrees of the [Second Vatican] Council, and drew attention to
issues of war and peace, poverty and development, and other matters
of social concern addressed in later papal encyclicals."[1]

Another long-standing Jesuit tradition, dating back to the time of
founder Saint Ignatius Loyola, is avoidance of personal publicity.
However, due to his prominent position as Superior General, Father
Arrupe's life is well-documented in both the Catholic and secular
presses. He was even featured on the cover of *TIME* magazine in April
1973. He also wrote prolifically, so we have a large corpus of his experience and insight. What is less documented, however, is the period
from 1981 to 1991, during which Father Arrupe became progressively
more and more disabled due to a severe stroke.

*Family and Early Life*
Arrupe was born in Bilbao, Spain, in 1907. He was the only son, the
youngest of five children. Pedro Arrupe describes his family as "very
close, very quiet, and very patriarchal in the Catholic sense."[2] His
father, an architect, had great devotion to the Sacred Heart, which
impressed his son greatly. His mother, a quiet and devout woman, died
when he was ten years old. At age fifteen Arrupe went to Madrid to
study medicine. Three years later his father died. After the death of
his father, Arrupe and his sisters traveled to Lourdes for a time of
quiet grieving together.

While at Lourdes, Arrupe was greatly impressed by the miraculous healing of a young man severely disabled with polio. During the

evening procession, Arrupe and his sisters watched as a bishop blessed the disabled young man with a monstrance: "He looked at the monstrance with the same faith with which the paralytic mentioned in the Gospel must have looked at Jesus. After the bishop had made the sign of the cross with the Blessed Sacrament, the young man rose cured from the cart, as the crowd filled with joy cried out: 'Miracle! Miracle!'"[3] Later, Arrupe, permitted as a medical student to work at the Office of Verification, realized that he had, indeed, witnessed a genuine miracle: "Thanks to the special permission which I had, I was later able to assist at the medical examinations. The Lord had truly cured him."[4] He continues: "I was filled with an immense joy. I seemed to be standing by the side of Jesus."[5] The incident was the beginning of Arrupe's vocation to the Jesuits: "Three months later I entered the novitiate of the Society of Jesus in Loyola, Spain."[6]

Because the Spanish Republic expelled all the Jesuits from Spain in 1932, Arrupe continued his formation studies in theology and medical ethics in Belgium and Holland. He was ordained to the priesthood on July 30, 1936, and went to the United States for his tertianship, or final Jesuit formation. Throughout his years in formation, he had felt God calling him to be a missionary. The Jesuits granted his request, sending him to Japan in 1938. Initially, Arrupe served as a parish priest; later, he was appointed Novice Master of the Japanese novices in Nagatsuka. Thus Arrupe was at center stage for one of the most horrific acts of the twentieth century: the dropping of the atomic bomb on Hiroshima.

*Hiroshima*

Fortunately, the Jesuit novitiate was located in Nagatsuka, a town several miles outside the city of Hiroshima. Almost immediately after the explosion, severely burned and wounded survivors began to straggle toward Nagatsuka. "I had studied medicine many years earlier, and I ran back to the house to find medical supplies. I found the medicine chest under some ruins with the door off its hinges. I retrieved some iodine, aspirins, and bicarbonate of soda. Those were the only supplies at a time when 200,000 victims needed help. What could I do? Where to begin? Again I fell on my knees and implored God's help."[7]

God's response was to inspire Arrupe to turn the novitiate building into a hospital. Arrupe and his novices did just that, heartbroken that they could care for only 150 survivors of the hundreds of thousands who required assistance. They dealt with an array of trauma: deep wounds in need of cleaning, pieces of wood and glass embedded in flesh, and serious burns of all types. Arrupe recalls: "The suffering was frightful, the pain excruciating, and it made bodies writhe like snakes, yet there was not a word of complaint. They all suffered in silence."[8]

Realizing that his patients would desperately need adequate food and water to survive, Arrupe sent some of his men to scavenge for food. Then God provided a minor miracle: More than thirty pounds of boric acid turned up. Arrupe and his novices tore up sheets for bandages, and were able to continually keep moist and clean their patients' wounds.

"Of the dead, fifty thousand died the moment of the explosion itself, another two hundred thousand during the following weeks, and others much later as a result of wounds or radiation," Arrupe writes. "We were, in effect, the first guinea pigs in such experimentation."[9] Fortunately, many of the people Arrupe and his Jesuits treated survived due to the good care.

*Reflections on Hiroshima*

As an eyewitness to Hiroshima, Arrupe was often called upon to share his reminiscences in later years. In 1970 Arrupe reflected not only on his recollections of the atomic explosion at Hiroshima, but also on what Father Kevin Burke describes as "a collective examination of conscience in the face of our troubled world."[10] Arrupe's prescient words ring all the more true today, in our post–September 11 world of terrorism, preemptive war and suicide bombings.

Writing that the threat of nuclear destruction continues to tor-ment humanity with its own destruction, Arrupe points out that political policies or ideologies may, in the long run, be even more destructive of human life than an atomic bomb: "Now yet another explosion is breeding in the womb of time, as millions die from hunger and subhuman existence.... Clearly the present world order is based neither on justice nor love, but almost always on personal and national interest."[11] And, in strong words, Arrupe is clear about the underlying reason: "Atomic disintegration would not have to be feared if it were not at the service of a humanity disintegrated by hate."[12] Arrupe is just as clear that firm, spiritual, Gospel-based values are the antidote to this hatred that afflicts the human race.

In order to avoid a "violent tearing down of unjust structures," Pedro points out the need for "striking personal conversion of those who have most influence to bring about the needed changes."[13] Thorough, profound conversion of heart will be needed on both a personal and national level if the human family is to survive: "History shows that neither war nor violent revolution have ever solved our problems; nor will they ever. They are born of hatred and, though hatred harms, it does not heal."[14]

In a powerful concluding metaphor, Pedro writes that modern sci-ence, specifically atomic physics, moves us toward the interior of mat-ter: "When will the day come on which humanity reaches the final stra-tum of matter and is able to glimpse...a new reality encased in all being: the divine reality? Above all, when will we discover that in the core of our person there lives that divine reality?"[15] It is only when we realize, like Caryll Houselander, that God is within every human being on the earth that we will stop hating one another, stop attacking one another, stop exploiting one another, and begin to turn hatred into the love for one another that Jesus so explicitly commanded us to have.

*Superior General*
Pedro Arrupe's life experience on several continents, as well as his abil-ity to articulate that experience in Gospel terms, uniquely qualified

him for his selection by his congregation as Superior General of the Society of Jesus in May 1965. Father Arrupe's initial reaction to this selection reflected the prophet Jeremiah: "*nescio loqui*—I do not know how to speak.' I had no qualifications, and I found myself facing the Society, its great scholars, its great doctors, its great spiritual masters.... My only assurance was, continuing to quote from Jeremiah: '...Be not afraid...for I am with you.' Without the Lord we can do nothing."[16]

Although Father Arrupe had personal reservations about leading this congregation of highly educated and diverse priests and brothers, his community had chosen well. With Vatican Council II the Catholic church was truly becoming a world church, and the Jesuits appreciated Arrupe's experience in Asia. His congregation was also aware of his deep attachment to their founder, Ignatius of Loyola, which would keep them rooted in their centuries-old tradition. On the other hand, the Jesuits knew, too, that "Don Pedro," as they affectionately referred to him, was open to the renewal being called for by the Council.

Father Kevin Burke describes Father Arrupe's tenure: "As the Superior General of the Jesuits during the period of renewal following Vatican II, Arrupe embodied a view of religious leadership rooted in collegiality, discernment, and service. He promoted the thoroughgoing renovation of the Society of Jesus, as the conciliar decree on religious life mandated, and his immediate impact on Jesuit religious life has been viewed as nothing short of a refounding of the order."[17]

Father Arrupe encountered obstacles both within and outside the Society of Jesus as he patiently steered his congregation toward renewal. Father Vincent O'Keefe, Father Arrupe's General Assistant throughout his generalate, describes Arrupe's efforts: "Don Pedro worked tirelessly to carry out Vatican II's mandate for renewal and adaptation to the changed conditions of the times. Fidelity, for him, meant change. Instead of a wooden and mindless repetition of what we had always done, he promoted spiritual discernment to read the signs of the times, to find God in all things, especially in our brothers and sisters in need, and in the major events and movements of the day."[18] Arrupe's tenure as Superior General of the Jesuits is often viewed not only as one of renewal for their congregation, but as one that steered them toward a firm and consistent "preferential option for the poor." For Don Pedro, this option for the poor peoples of the world included a special emphasis on refugees through the establishment of the Jesuit Refugee Service (JRS) in 1989. The JRS serves in more than fifty countries worldwide and performed outstanding service in the Indian Ocean tsunami crisis of 2004.

In addition to his profound impact on the Jesuit congregation, Pedro Arrupe's tenure as Superior General helped shape the post–Vatican II church: "As Superior General of the Jesuits from May 22, 1965, until he was disabled by a stroke on August 7, 1981, he was intimately associated with many officials of the Church's curia in Rome, with Bishops from all the world, with Superiors General of many religious institutes of women and men, and with other important persons of ecclesiastical and civil life. Thus he had a role of no small importance in shaping the thought currents and other developments of the post-Conciliar era."[19] Father Arrupe was also elected five times in succession as President of the Union of Superiors General, serving a total of fifteen years in that post.

*Arrupe and Ignatius*

All Jesuits are called to model their lives on that of Saint Ignatius Loyola, the famed mystic and founder of their congregation. Pedro Arrupe, however, had a special affinity for Ignatius. Like Ignatius, Arrupe was Basque. Arrupe's novitiate period took place next to the residence of the Loyola family, where Ignatius had his early spiritual experiences and conversion. Arrupe shared with his founder a deep reverence for the Eucharist. Also, Arrupe was steeped in the writings of Ignatius and recognized how crucial it was for the Society of Jesus to live out of the charism of Ignatius himself: "We must reincarnate this charism, not by rummaging through the centuries and the thoughts and deeds of the Jesuits during those centuries, but by seeking out anew St. Ignatius."[20] Don Pedro's deep love of "Father Ignatius" endeared him greatly to his fellow Jesuits.

Pedro Arrupe's life clearly reflected the life of the founder of the Jesuits. Like Ignatius, Arrupe strove continually to find God in all things, to live his life in service to the church, and to be a close companion of Jesus carrying his cross. For Don Pedro, the cross of Jesus grew considerably heavier on an August day in 1981.

*Stroke*

It happened quite suddenly, as it usually does. Pedro Arrupe was returning to Rome from a visit to the Philippines. After disembarking from the plane, Don Pedro began perspiring heavily and had difficulty closing his hand around his luggage. He also began to speak rather incoherently in English. His companion, American Father Robert Rush, immediately rushed him to the Salvator Mundi Hospital for treatment.

Father O'Keefe, upon hearing that the Jesuit General had been taken to the hospital, immediately left the Jesuit residence. The prognosis was grim from the beginning:

> The stroke affected the left side of the brain, paralyzing him on his right side. He couldn't use his right arm and needed a brace on his right leg. The stroke affected the area of the brain that controls language; he had trouble talking, and couldn't read any more. Over the remaining ten years of his life, he gradually lost his ability to speak other languages, including English. By the end he was having difficulty even in speaking his native Spanish. That stroke took him from a highly independent, self-sufficient person to someone who was completely dependent on others.[21]

Indeed, Father Arrupe's independence was legendary: He had even insisted on doing his own laundry. Sadly, his days of self-sufficiency were now ended forever.

The brain is a complex organ: It is the control panel for every aspect of the human person. When any brain cells do not receive the oxygen the blood normally carries to them, the result is a stroke. There are two types of stroke: brain hemorrhage, bleeding of the brain; and brain ischemia, when adequate blood does not flow to all portions of the brain. A stroke adversely affects a person physically, mentally and emotionally. When the left side of the brain has lost oxygen, the right side of the body is damaged, and vice versa. Some strokes are relatively minor; others, as in Pedro Arrupe's case, can be life-changing.

Stroke is the third leading cause of death in the United States, killing approximately 275,000 Americans a year. Risk for stroke increases with age: nearly two-thirds of all strokes occur in people over age sixty-five.[22]

Fortunately, there are more treatment options available today than there were for Pedro Arrupe in 1981. In addition to medications, surgical procedures are available both to prevent, as well as treat, strokes.

How difficult it must have been for this man who was Superior General of the Jesuit order, who enjoyed traveling and meeting people all over the world, who had such an impact on renewal in the Catholic church after Vatican II, whose Jesuit spirit was so infectious that it made his men proud to be Jesuits, to be slowly stripped of his ability to think, reason and communicate in any way. In addition to all this, Father Arrupe needed assistance with basic activities of daily living, such as bathing, dressing and eating.

After Pedro Arrupe left Salvator Mundi Hospital in September 1981, he moved to the Jesuit infirmary, where Brother Raphael Bandera became his personal-care assistant until his death on February 5, 1991. Father O'Keefe and the other assistants continued to visit him there. As Don Pedro was unable to read, his assistants had to speak directly to him. He would nod in affirmation or shake his head in disagreement. On August 10, 1981, Father Arrupe appointed Father O'Keefe to govern the Society of Jesus for the duration of his illness.

As we have seen time and time again throughout this book, God provides the grace necessary to deal with whatever setback life brings. Pedro Arrupe lived heroically despite his severely diminished capabilities from his stroke. Although his language-speaking abilities slowly declined, Don Pedro was still able to communicate with someone face-to-face. His silent acceptance and refusal to complain about his condition moved and strengthened the Jesuits who attended him, and ultimately moved and strengthened the entire Jesuit congregation. Indeed, Father O'Keefe believes that in the mystical, mysterious way that graced suffering heals the Body of Christ, Pedro Arrupe's ten years of living with his stroke accomplished as much for the Society of Jesus and the church as any of the remarkable accomplishments of his generalate.

*"I Am Still the Apostle"*
When Pedro Arrupe had visited Jesuit communities around the world, he had always made sure to visit infirmaries and hospitals. While meeting with the priests and brothers who were elders or ill, Arrupe would always urge them to remind themselves, "I am still the apostle." He stressed that even though they could no longer give retreats, teach or participate in other active ministries, they still had an apostolate—the apostolate of prayer. "Prayer is the big thing," he would emphasize, "it's not all action, action, action."[23] Their Superior General's presence to them, as well as his message that prayer is the foundational apostolate, meant a great deal to the Jesuit elders and ill members.

Father Arrupe's years of prayer, devotion to Eucharist and concern for Jesuit elders and ill members perhaps prepared him spiritually to live with the slow diminishment of his powers due to his stroke. No doubt his witnessing and tending to the great suffering of the survivors of Hiroshima also helped him when his moment of walking ever more closely with Jesus arrived in August 1981. He, too, must now utter those privileged yet difficult words: "I am just as apostolic now as I have ever been." Don Pedro, for years minister to the world's wounded, was now grievously wounded himself. He now needed to reach deep, to unite his own pain and loss with what he had witnessed among humanity's marginalized masses.

*Amen, Alleluia*
Anyone familiar with Ignatius of Loyola knows about "Ignatian indifference," the concept laid out so beautifully in the Principle and Foundation prayer that begins the Spiritual Exercises: "In everyday life, then, we must hold ourselves in balance before all these created gifts insofar as we have a choice and are not bound by some obligation. We should not fix our desires on health or sickness, wealth or poverty, success or failure, a long life or short one. *For everything has the potential of calling forth in us a deeper response to our life in God.*"[24]

*Everything:* Those reflective moments in church, contemplating the beauty of God's creation from a mountaintop, the thrill of a newborn child, as well as life's struggles: losing someone dear to us, struggling with an addiction or disability or, like Pedro Arrupe, having a severe stroke. Ignatius of Loyola made himself very clear: He invited us to hold all things in life lightly in our hands. We are, of course, to appreciate God's gifts of health, success, wealth or a long life, but we are not to cling to these gifts, even to our own lives. For *every* single condition in life, no matter how difficult, has the potential of bringing us closer to God. We, of course, must recognize the opportunity for grace in *everything,* especially in the more difficult aspects of our lives.

This is a profound grace to pray for. Note that Ignatius is *not* saying to request hard things in life; however, when the raindrops of adversity start pelting our heads, we are invited to view them as an opportunity to draw close to God. Obviously, in our humanity, we want things to go smoothly for ourselves and our loved ones.

However, perhaps we can turn the bad into good by letting our struggles unite us with the cross of Jesus. We can learn to depend less on ourselves and more on God. This is especially true when illness or disability enters our lives abruptly, as it did with Pedro Arrupe.

Don Pedro's favorite prayer had always been "Amen, Alleluia!" By the "Amen" he meant, "I accept all that has gone before"; by "Alleluia," "I accept all that will be in the future."[25] Now, after serving in the highest position in his congregation, after helping the worldwide church move toward the renewal called for by Vatican II, Pedro Arrupe needed this prayer of detachment more than ever before. The Superior General who had exhorted his fellow Jesuits, "Prayer is the big thing; it's not all action, action, action," now had the opportunity to realize this himself.

### God's Hands

After Father Arrupe's stroke, the governance and administrative affairs of the worldwide Jesuit congregation still had to be attended to. Father Vincent O'Keefe, in close contact with Pedro Arrupe, administered the Jesuit congregation until October 5, 1981, when Pope John Paul II, in an unexpected move, sent an Italian Jesuit, Paolo Dezza, to be his personal delegate to govern the Society. The situation remained like this until the Jesuits elected Father Peter-Hans Kolvenbach as their new Superior General at the Thirty-Third General Congregation in 1983.

At this Thirty-Third General Congregation, the Jesuit delegates heard their beloved Don Pedro's words once again. Father Arrupe had managed to convey what he wanted to say in his final address as Superior General to Father O'Keefe and his other general assistants. His words were read to the delegates by Father Ignacio Iglesias: "More than ever, I now find myself in the hands of God. This is what I have wanted all my life, from my youth. And this is still the one thing I want.... It is indeed a profound spiritual experience to know and feel myself so totally in his hands."[26] Arrupe ended his address with the famed Ignatian *Suscipe*, "Take, O Lord, and receive all my liberty, my memory, my understanding and my whole will."[27] No prayer could have been more fitting. The Jesuits present leapt to their feet, giving their former Superior General a lengthy standing ovation.

The next day, Pedro Arrupe delivered his final homily to his congregation in the chapel at La Storta, a site of crucial importance to Jesuits. Comparing himself to Simeon in the Gospel, Pedro sang his own *Nunc Dimittis*, "Master, now you are dismissing your servant in peace" (Luke 2:29). He echoed the theme of the preceding day: "And now more than ever I find myself in the hands of this God who has taken hold of me."[28]

*Pedro as Companion*

"Ask, and it will be given to you," Jesus tells us (Luke 11:9). Yes, Don Pedro Arrupe had a lifetime of prayer behind him, which undoubtedly helped him deal with his sudden and severe incapacitation. However, God is lavish with grace and will always respond when we ask for help. It may not be the way we want—we may not leap out of bed healed and happy, but God will assist us, strengthen us interiorly and help us to deal with our lives one day, even one hour, at a time. God loves us deeply and weeps with us in our pain. Saint Paul tells us that God "consoles us in all our affliction, so that we may be able to console those who are in any affliction with the consolation with which we ourselves are consoled by God" (2 Corinthians 1:4). When we open our hearts to him, God will not disappoint.

And Don Pedro Arrupe is also there to help us. Whatever intense suffering we may experience, even that of stroke or other debilitating illness, we know that we have a friend among the communion of saints, a friend who has also lived with this type of illness. Experiencing disability as the result of a stroke certainly does not seem "holy." However, it is when we turn to God in our powerlessness, when we can be aware, as Pedro Arrupe was, of the tremendous spiritual power of detachment, of acknowledging God's presence in *every* life situation, that we are sanctifying our illness or disability. Pedro Arrupe knew the importance of leaning on God and was able to offer the severe suffering of his stroke for others. He stands as a giant among the communion of saints, cheering us on and inviting us to turn to him, to talk to him, to pour out our hearts to one who has been there, who understands, who continually reminded his men, "I am just as apostolic now as ever before."

And to this we say: Amen! Alleluia!

# bibliography

Al-Anon Family Groups. *From Survival to Recovery: Growing Up in an Alcoholic Home.* Virginia Beach, Va.: Al-Anon Family Headquarters, 1994.

Alcoholics Anonymous. *Twelve Steps and Twelve Traditions.* New York: Alcoholics Anonymous World Services, 2002.

*Almost Home: Living With Suffering and Dying.* VHS. Directed by David Howard. Liguori, Mo.: Redemptorist Pastoral Communications, 1989.

Arrupe, Pedro. *One Jesuit's Spiritual Journey: Autobiographical Conversations with Jean-Claude Dietsch, S.J.* Ruth Bradley, trans. St. Louis: The Institute of Jesuit Sources, 1986.

———. *Pedro Arrupe: Essential Writings.* Kevin Burke, ed. Maryknoll, N.Y.: Orbis, 2004.

Bernardin, Joseph. *The Gift of Peace.* Chicago: Loyola, 1997.

Bonniwell, William R. *The Life of Blessed Margaret of Castello.* Rockford, Ill.: Tan Books, 1952.

Bowman, Thea. *Sister Thea Bowman, Shooting Star: Selected Writings and Speeches.* Celestine Cepress, ed. La Crosse, Wis.: Franciscan Sisters of Perpetual Adoration, 1999.

Bunson, Margaret R. *Kateri Tekakwitha: Mystic of the Wilderness.* Huntington, Ind.: Our Sunday Visitor, 1998.

Butler, Alban. *Butler's Lives of the Saints.* Mineola, N.Y.: Dover, 2005.

Catherine of Genoa. *The Life and Sayings of Catherine of Genoa.* Paul Garvin, ed. New York: Alba House, 1964.

Clarke, John, trans. *St. Thérèse of Lisieux: Her Last Conversations.* Washington, D.C.: Institute of Carmelite Studies Publications, 1973.

Ellsberg, Robert. *All Saints: Daily Reflections on Saints, Prophets, and Witnesses for Our Time.* New York: Crossroad, 1997.

Flinders, Carol Lee. *Enduring Grace: Living Portraits of Seven Women Mystics.* New York: HarperCollins, 1993.

Görres, Ida Friederike. *The Hidden Face: A Study of St. Thérèse of Lisieux.* Richard and Clara Winston, trans. New York: Pantheon, 1959.

Houselander, Caryll. *A Rocking-Horse Catholic.* New York: Sheed and Ward, 1955.

————. *The Way of the Cross.* New York: Sheed and Ward, 1955.

Hughes, Serge, trans. *Catherine of Genoa: Purgation and Purgatory, The Spiritual Dialogue.* New York: Paulist Press, 1979.

Ignatius of Loyola. *The Autobiography of St. Ignatius of Loyola.* Joseph O'Callaghan, trans. New York: Fordham University Press, 1992.

Johnson, Elizabeth A. *Friends of God and Prophets: A Feminist Theological Reading of the Communion of Saints.* New York: Continuum, 1998.

Julian of Norwich. *Revelations of Divine Love.* Roger L. Roberts, ed. Wilton, Conn.: Morehouse-Barlow, 1982.

Kennedy, Eugene. *My Brother Joseph: The Spirit of a Cardinal and the Story of a Friendship.* New York: St. Martin's, 1997.

LaRochester, Barbara. "She Walked by Faith and Not by Sight." In *Thea Bowman: Handing on Her Legacy,* Christian Koontz, ed. Kansas City: Sheed and Ward, 1991.

Maynard, Philip. *To Slake a Thirst: The Matt Talbot Way to Sobriety.* New York: Alba House, 2000.

Meissner, W.W. *Ignatius of Loyola: The Psychology of a Saint.* New Haven, Conn.: Yale University Press, 1992.

*New Catholic Encyclopedia, second edition.* Washington, D.C.: The Catholic University of America, 2002.

Puhl, John, trans. *The Spiritual Exercises of St. Ignatius.* New York: Vintage, 2000.

Purcell, Mary. *Matt Talbot and His Times*. Dublin: M.H. Gill and Son, 1954.

Sargent, Daniel R. *Catherine Tekakwitha*. New York: Longmans, Green and Co., 1936.

Savage, Anne, and Nicholas Watson, trans. *Anchoritic Spirituality: Ancrene Wisse and Associated Works*. Mahwah: N.J.: Paulist, 1991.

*Sr. Thea: Her Own Story*. VHS. Directed by Aaron Mermelstein. Washington, DC: United States Catholic Conference, Oblate Media and Communication Campaign, 1988.

Thérèse of Lisieux. *Story of a Soul: The Autobiography of St. Therese of Lisieux*, John Clarke, trans. Washington, D.C.: Institute of Carmelite Studies Publications, 1976.

Ward, Maisie. *Caryll Houselander: That Divine Eccentric*. New York: Sheed and Ward, 1962.

——, ed. *The Letters of Caryll Houselander: Her Spiritual Legacy*. New York: Sheed and Ward, 1965.

Wilson, Lois. *Lois Remembers: Memoirs of the Co-founder of Al-Anon and Wife of the Co-founder of Alcoholics Anonymous*. Virginia Beach, Va.: Al-Anon Family Group Headquarters, 1979.

Woodward, Kenneth L. *Making Saints: How the Catholic Church Determines Who Becomes a Saint, Who Doesn't, and Why*. New York: Touchstone, 1996.

# notes

NOTE TO READERS

1. Elizabeth A. Johnson, *Friends of God and Prophets: A Feminist Theological Reading of the Communion of Saints* (New York: Continuum, 1998), p. 19.

2. Johnson, p. 7.

3. Johnson, p. 81.

TWO : JULIAN OF NORWICH

1. Julian of Norwich, *Revelations of Divine Love*. Roger L. Roberts, ed. (Wilton, Conn.: Morehouse-Barlow, 1982), p. 8.

2. Julian of Norwich, p. 8.

3. Julian of Norwich, p. 8.

4. Julian of Norwich, pp. 8–9.

5. Anne Savage and Nicholas Watson, trans. *Anchorite Spirituality: Ancrene Wisse and Associated Works* (Mahwah, N.J.: Paulist, 1991), p. 206.

6. Savage and Watson, p. 202.

7. Savage and Watson, p. 206.

8. Savage and Watson, p. 206.

9. Savage and Watson, p. 207.

10. Carol Lee Flinders, *Enduring Grace: Living Portraits of Seven Women Mystics* (New York: HarperCollins, 1993), p. 80.

11. Savage and Watson, p. 176.

12. Julian of Norwich, p. 10.

13. Julian of Norwich, p. 10.

14. Julian of Norwich, p. 10.

15. Julian of Norwich, p. 10.

16. Julian of Norwich, p. 10.

17. Julian of Norwich, p. 11.

18. Julian of Norwich, p. 12.

19. Julian of Norwich, p. 12.

20. Julian of Norwich, p. 12.

21. Julian of Norwich, p. 13.

22. Julian of Norwich, p. 19.

23. Julian of Norwich, p. 33.

THREE : CATHERINE OF GENOA

1. National Center on Caregiving, "Fact Sheet: Women and Caregiving: Facts and Figures" (San Francisco: Family Caregiver Alliance, 2003), http://www.caregiver.org/caregiver/jsp/content_ node.jsp?nodeid=892.

2. National Center on Caregiving.

3. Prayer attributed to Saint Teresa of Avila.

4. Flinders, p. 136.

5. F.M. Capes, "St. Catherine of Genoa," John Looby, trans. (Catholic Encyclopedia Online Edition, 2005), http://www.newadvent.org/ cathen/03446b.htm.

6. Catherine of Genoa, The Life and Sayings of St. Catherine of Genoa, Paul Garvin, ed. (New York: Alba House, 1964), p. 24.

7. Capes.

8. Flinders, p. 140.

9. Serge Hughes, trans. Catherine of Genoa: Purgation and Purgatory, The Spiritual Dialogue (Mahwah, N.J.: Paulist, 1979), pp. 128–129.

10. Hughes, p. 129.

11. Hughes, pp. 129–130.

12. Hughes, p. 131.

13. Flinders, p. 150.

14. Catherine of Genoa, p. 34.

15. Flinders, p. 151.

16. Hughes, p. 134.

17. Hughes, p. 135.

18. Flinders, p. 149.

19. Catherine of Genoa, p. 69.

20. Lisa Birnbach, "Do Something For Someone" *Parade* May 1, 2005: pp. 6–7.

21. Catherine of Genoa, p. 69.

22. "The Future Supply of Long-Term Care Workers in Relation to the Aging Baby Boom Generation." Report to Congress. May 14, 2003. http://aspe.hhs.gov/daltcp/reports/ltcwork.htm#section1.

FOUR : SAINT IGNATIUS OF LOYOLA

1. Ignatius of Loyola, *The Autobiography of St. Ignatius Loyola*, Joseph F. O'Callaghan, trans. (New York: Fordham University Press, 1992), p. 21.

2. W.W. Meissner, *Ignatius of Loyola: The Psychology of a Saint* (New Haven, Conn.: Yale University, 1992), p. 22.

3. Ignatius of Loyola, p. 21.

4. Ignatius of Loyola, p. 22.

5. Ignatius of Loyola, p. 22.

6. Ignatius of Loyola, p. 22.

7. Ignatius of Loyola, p. 22.

8. Ignatius of Loyola, p. 22.

9. Ignatius of Loyola, p. 23.

10. Ignatius of Loyola, p. 23.

11. Ignatius of Loyola, p. 24.

12. Ignatius of Loyola, p. 24.

13. Ignatius of Loyola, p. 24.

14. Ignatius of Loyola, p. 24

15. Ignatius of Loyola, p. 25.

## FIVE : BLESSED KATERI TEKAKWITHA

1. Margaret R. Bunson, *Kateri Tekakwitha: Mystic of the Wilderness* (Huntington, Ind.: Our Sunday Visitor, 1992), p. 33.

2. Bunson, p. 43.

3. Bunson, p. 89.

4. Bunson, p. 97.

5. Daniel Sargent, *Catherine Tekakwitha* (New York: Longmans, Green and Co., 1936), p. 242.

## SIX : SAINT THÉRÈSE OF LISIEUX

1. Ida Friederike Görres, *The Hidden Face: A Study of St. Thérèse of Lisieux*, Richard and Clara Winston, trans. (New York: Pantheon, 1959), p. 352.

2. Thérèse of Lisieux, *Story of a Soul: The Autobiography of St. Thérèse of Lisieux*, John Clarke, trans. (Washington, D.C.: Institute of Carmelite Studies Publications, 1976), p. 210.

3. Thérèse of Lisieux, p. 211.

4. Görres, p. 364.

5. John Clarke, trans. *St. Thérèse of Lisieux: Her Last Conversations* (Washington, D.C.: Institute of Carmelite Studies Publications, 1977), p. 50.

6. Clarke, p. 149.

7. Clarke, p. 284.

8. Thérèse of Lisieux, p. 210.

9. Thérèse of Lisieux, p. 149.

10. Clarke, p. 129.

11. Louis J. Puhl, trans., *The Spiritual Exercises of St. Ignatius* (New York: Vintage, 2000), p. 12.

12. Clarke, p. 132.

13. Clarke, p. 133.

14. Clarke, p. 57.

15. Clarke, p. 112.

16. Clarke, p. 62.

17. Clarke, p. 167.

18. Clarke, p. 206.

19. Clarke, p. 62.

SEVEN : VENERABLE MATT TALBOT

1. Mary Purcell, *Matt Talbot and His Times* (Dublin: M.H. Gill and Son, 1954), p. 44.

2. Purcell, p. 47.

3. Purcell, p. 50.

4. Purcell, p. 53.

5. Purcell, p. 52.

6. Purcell, p. 66.

7. Purcell, p. 53.

8. Al-Anon Family Groups, *The Twelve Steps and Traditions* (Virginia Beach, Va.: Al-Anon Family Headquarters, 1986), p. 3.

9. Al-Anon Family Groups, p. 3.

10. Al-Anon Family Groups, p. 3.

11. Purcell, p. 91.

12. Purcell, p. 49.

13. Purcell, p. 64.

14. Lois Wilson, *Lois Remembers: Memoirs of the Co-founder of Al-Anon and Wife of the Co-founder of Alcoholics Anonymous* (Virginia Beach, Va.: Al-Anon Family Group Headquarters, 1979), preface.

15. The National Council on Alcoholism and Drug Dependence, "Alcoholism and Drug Dependence Are America's Number One Health Problem," http://www.ncadd.org/facts/numberoneprob.html.

16. Al-Anon Family Groups, *From Survival to Recovery: Growing Up in an Alcoholic Home* (Virginia Beach, Va.: Al-Anon Family Headquarters, 1994), p. 17.

EIGHT : CARYLL HOUSELANDER

1. Maisie Ward, ed. *The Letters of Caryll Houselander: Her Spiritual Legacy* (New York: Sheed and Ward, 1965), p. 183.

2. *The Letters of Caryll Houselander*, p. 156.

3. *The Letters of Caryll Houselander*, p. 227.

4. *The Letters of Caryll Houselander*, p. 232.

5. *The Letters of Caryll Houselander*, p. 209.

6. Caryll Houselander, *A Rocking-Horse Catholic*, (New York: Sheed and Ward, 1955), pp. 135–136.

7. *A Rocking-Horse Catholic*, p. 137.

8. *A Rocking-Horse Catholic*, p. 138.

9. *A Rocking-Horse Catholic*, p. 139.

10. *A Rocking-Horse Catholic*, p. 137.

11. *The Letters of Caryll Houselander*, p. 139.

12. *The Letters of Caryll Houselander*, p. 226.

13. *The Letters of Caryll Houselander*, pp. 91–92.

14. *The Letters of Caryll Houselander*, p. 92.

15. *The Letters of Caryll Houselander*, p. 221.

16. Maisie Ward, *Caryll Houselander: That Divine Eccentric* (New York: Sheed and Ward, 1962), p. 264.

17. *That Divine Eccentric*, p. 278.

18. *The Letters of Caryll Houselander*, p. 183.

19. *The Letters of Caryll Houselander*, p. 111.

20. *The Letters of Caryll Houselander*, p. 212.

21. *The Letters of Caryll Houselander*, p. 214.

22. *The Letters of Caryll Houselander*, pp. 214–215.

23. Caryll Houselander, *The Way of the Cross* (New York: Sheed and Ward, 1955), p. 26.

24. Houselander, p. 47.

NINE : CARDINAL JOSEPH BERNARDIN

1. Joseph Bernardin, *The Gift of Peace* (Chicago: Loyola, 1997), p. 87.

2. Bernardin, p. 5.

3. Bernardin, p. 5.

4. Bernardin, p. 6.

5. Eugene Kennedy, *My Brother Joseph: The Spirit of a Cardinal and the Story of a Friendship* (New York: St. Martin's, 1997), p. 105.

6. Kennedy, p. 108.

7. Kennedy, pp. 109–110.

8. Bernardin, p. 26.

9. Bernardin, p. 27.

10. Bernardin, p. 28.

11. Bernardin, p. 24.

12. Bernardin, p. 30.

13. Bernardin, p. 34.

14. Bernardin, p. 71.

15. Bernardin, p. 95.

16. Bernardin, p. 75.

17. Kennedy, pp. 138–139.

18. Kennedy, p. 142.

19. Bernardin, p. 109.

20. Bernardin, p. 96.

21. Kennedy, p. 150.

22. Bernardin, pp. 97–98.

23. Bernardin, p. 3.

24. Bernardin, p. 126.

25. Bernardin, pp. 152–153.

Ten : Sister Thea Bowman

1. *Almost Home: Living With Suffering and Dying,* VHS, directed by David Howard (1989; Liguori, Mo.: Redemptorist Pastoral Communications).

2. *Almost Home.*

3. Thea Bowman, *Sister Thea Bowman, Shooting Star: Selected Writings and Speeches,* Celestine Cepress, PH.D., ed., in collaboration with Carl Koch (La Crosse: Wis.: Franciscan Sisters of Perpetual Adoration, 1999), p. 17.

4. Bowman, p. 18.

5. *Sr. Thea: Her Own Story,* VHS, directed by Aaron Mermelstein (1988; Washington, D.C.: United States Catholic Conference Oblate Media and Communication Campaign).

6. Marla Lang phone interview with author, March 31, 2005.

7. Marla Lang, phone interview.

8. Jean Kasparbauer, e-mail to author, April 18, 2005.

9. Jean Kasparbauer e-mail to author.

10. Bowman, p. 26.

11. *Almost Home.*

12. *Sr. Thea, Her Own Story.*

13. Bowman, p. 26.

14. Charlene Smith, e-mail to author.

15. *Sr. Thea, Her Own Story.*

16. *Sr. Thea, Her Own Story.*

17. *Sr. Thea, Her Own Story.*

18. Barbara LaRochester, "She Walked by Faith and Not by Sight," *Thea Bowman: Handing on Her Legacy,* Christian Koontz, ed. (Kansas City: Sheed and Ward, 1991), p. 47.

19. Dorothy Kundinger, phone interview with author, March 25, 2005.

20. Bowman, p. 29.

21. Bowman, p. 32.

22. Bowman, p. 32.

23. *Almost Home.*

24. Dorothy Kundinger, phone interview.

25. Marla Lang, phone interview.

26. *Almost Home.*

27. *Almost Home.*

28. *Almost Home.*

29. Bowman, p. 128.

30. *Almost Home.*

31. Bowman, p. 126.

32. Bowman, p. 127.

33. Dorothy Kundinger, phone interview.

34. Bowman, p. 129.

ELEVEN : PEDRO ARRUPE

1. Pedro Arrupe, *Pedro Arrupe: Essential Writings*, Kevin F. Burke, ed. (Maryknoll, N.Y.: Orbis, 2004), p. 21.

2. Pedro Arrupe, *One Jesuit's Spiritual Journey: Autobiographical Conversations with Jean-Claude Dietsch, S.J.*, Ruth Bradley, trans. (St. Louis: Institute of Jesuit Sources, 1986), p. 49.

3. *Pedro Arrupe: Essential Writings*, p. 53.

4. *Pedro Arrupe: Essential Writings*, p. 53.

5. *Pedro Arrupe: Essential Writings*, p. 53.

6. *Pedro Arrupe: Essential Writings*, p. 53.

7. *Pedro Arrupe: Essential Writings*, p. 41.

8. *Pedro Arrupe: Essential Writings*, p. 43.

9. *Pedro Arrupe: Essential Writings*, p. 50.

10. *Pedro Arrupe: Essential Writings*, p. 187.

11. *Pedro Arrupe: Essential Writings*, p. 190.

12. *Pedro Arrupe: Essential Writings*, p. 188.

13. *Pedro Arrupe: Essential Writings*, p. 191.

14. *Pedro Arrupe: Essential Writings*, pp. 195–196.

15. *Pedro Arrupe: Essential Writings*, p. 196.

16. *One Jesuit's Spiritual Journey*, p. 22.

17. *Pedro Arrupe: Essential Writings*, p. 21.

18. Vincent O'Keefe, "The Creative Fidelity of Pedro Arrupe," *America*, December 20, 1997, pp. 4–6.

19. George E. Ganss, ed, *Pedro Arrupe: One Jesuit's Spiritual Journey: Autobiographical Conversations with Jean-Claude Dietsch, S.J.*, p. vii.

20. *One Jesuit's Spiritual Journey*, p. 46.

21. Vincent O'Keefe, phone interview with author, May 11, 2005.

22. http://www.strokecenter.org/pat/stats.htm.

23. Vincent O'Keefe, phone interview.

24. Ignatius of Loyola as paraphrased by David L. Fleming, *Hearts on Fire: Praying with Jesuits*, Michael Harter, ed. (St Louis: Institute of Jesuit Sources, 1993), p. 9, emphasis added.

25. Vincent O'Keefe, phone interview.

26. *Pedro Arrupe: Essential Writings*, p. 201.

27. *Pedro Arrupe: Essential Writings*, p. 203.

28. *Pedro Arrupe: Essential Writings*, p. 204.